THE NORMAN WAIT HARRIS MEMORIAL FOUNDATION

THE Harris Foundation Lectures at the University of Chicago have been made possible through the generosity of the heirs of Norman Wait Harris and Emma Gale Harris, who donated to the University a fund to be known as "The Norman Wait Harris Memorial Foundation" on January 27, 1923. The letter of gift contains the following statement:

It is apparent that a knowledge of world-affairs was never of more importance to Americans than today. The spirit of distrust which pervades the Old World is not without its effect upon our own country. How to combat this disintegrating tendency is a problem worthy of the most serious thought. Perhaps one of the best methods is the promotion of a better understanding of other nations through wisely directed educational effort.

The purpose of the foundation shall be the promotion of a better understanding on the part of American citizens of the other peoples of the world, thus establishing a basis for improved international relations and a more enlightened world-order. The aim shall always be to give accurate information, not to propagate opinion.

Annual Institutes have been held at the University of Chicago since the summer of 1924. The lectures delivered each year have been published in essentially their original form in a series of volumes of which this is the most recent.

INTER-AMERICAN SOLIDARITY

THE UNIVERSITY OF CHICAGO PRESS
CHICAGO, ILLINOIS

*

THE BAKER & TAYLOR COMPANY
NEW YORK

THE CAMBRIDGE UNIVERSITY PRESS
LONDON

[LECTURES ON THE HARRIS FOUNDATION 1941]

INTER-AMERICAN SOLIDARITY

by

HERMINIO PORTELL VILÁ, *Professor of History of the Americas, University of Havana;* GEORGE FIELDING ELIOT, *Military Critic, formerly Major, Military Intelligence Reserve, U.S. Army;* EDUARDO VILLASEÑOR, *Director, Banco de México, Mexico City;* ARTHUR R. UPGREN, *Professor of Economics, University of Minnesota;* FRANK SCOTT, *Professor of Civil Law, McGill University;* DANIEL SAMPER ORTEGA, *President, Gimnasio Moderno, Bogotá, Colombia;* J. FRED RIPPY, *Professor of American History, The University of Chicago*

WALTER H. C. LAVES, *Editor*

THE UNIVERSITY OF CHICAGO PRESS
CHICAGO · ILLINOIS

COMPOSED AND PRINTED BY THE UNIVERSITY OF CHICAGO PRESS
CHICAGO, ILLINOIS, U.S.A.

PREFACE

AMONG the many effects which the second World War has had within the Western Hemisphere is a very obviously increased concern about inter-American relations. This concern is reflected in government and private activity to create what is usually referred to as inter-American solidarity. The term "inter-American solidarity" as currently used embodies at one and the same time an implied recognition of the inadequacies of past relations among the American states, a fear for the security of these states in the rapidly deteriorating world situation, and a hope for a new order in the Western Hemisphere.

With an eye to the past, the phrase "inter-American solidarity" is intended to convey a change from the old Pan-Americanism. The latter meant, in practice, and with few exceptions until the inauguration of the good-neighbor policy, a Western Hemisphere ordered after the wishes of the United States, which assumed for itself a guiding and determining role. Pan-Americanism thus came to be nearly synonymous with "Pan–United Statesism," and there developed throughout the other American states a feeling of both fear and antagonism toward the "colossus of the north." In contrast to this conception of inter-American relations, the present one of inter-American solidarity suggests identity of interest, unity of purpose, and co-operation among equals.

In terms of the present world situation, the words "inter-American solidarity" call attention to the common danger which the American states face from the organized forces of fascist aggression and the need for a united resistance if individual American states are to preserve their independence.

Finally, the phrase "inter-American solidarity" carries in it the hope that there may be built in the future a more stable order in the Western Hemisphere—an order firmly based on the economic, social, and political interests of all states concerned. Whether this order is to be part of a world order or one of several regional orders, its objective is the enhancement of the welfare of the peoples of this hemisphere.

The achievement of inter-American solidarity becomes a particularly difficult problem because of the necessity of doing quickly and consciously what might be more easily done gradually and unconsciously. The undoing of past errors and the setting of new standards and objectives for inter-American relations must be undertaken now in the shadow of war and under the threat of impending conflict. Mutual suspicion, born of years of experience, must be replaced almost immediately by mutual confidence based principally on faith. A group of nations whose existence has been largely atomistic and which, for the most part, have been more concerned with east-west than with north-south contacts suddenly finds need for building a more intimate set of relationships.

The creation of a sense of solidarity among the American states requires an understanding of what they have in common and also of the existing barriers to mutual understanding. What is the cultural background of the various peoples of the Western Hemisphere; what are the values, standards, and beliefs by which they live? More than this, what are the economic implications of a more integrated social order in this hemisphere? What does this mean for the productive system of each country? Is the industrial superiority of the United States to be maintained or are the heretofore quasi-colonial economies of Latin-American states to be speeded into a condition of industrialization? What will be done to account for disparities in working and living conditions and in wages and hours? Must economic planning for the Americas be undertaken? If so, what shall be the contemplated relationship between the Western Hemisphere and the world outside?

More extensive relations among the peoples of this hemisphere similarly call for more comprehensive intergovernmental relations, quite aside from the expansion of government activity occasioned by the effort to encourage inter-American solidarity. Inevitably, this means new inter-American institutions. What shall be their character? How much more comprehensive shall they be than those now existing under the Pan-American Union and those created by the present emergency? Shall there be a League of American Nations or a new Federal Union? What shall be the relation between this new organization and the obviously needed world-wide organization?

Finally, recognizing that the problem of the Americas is today in part short run and in part long run, what immediate steps shall be taken for the common defense? Can sufficient real co-operation be secured to assure the preservation of the independence of all the American states, in spite of Latin-American fears of a future revival of United States imperialism?

These and many related issues must be faced in any realistic approach to the problem of inter-American solidarity. In the hope that it might, through its deliberations, throw some light upon them, the Seventeenth Institute under the Norman Wait Harris Memorial Foundation took as its subject "The Political and Economic Implications of Inter-American Solidarity." As in past years, the Institute consisted of round-table conferences and lectures. The former were attended by a limited number of experts in the fields affected by the topic

PREFACE

under discussion. The lectures were open to the public without restriction. The lectures, substantially as given, are made available in this volume, and it is hoped that they may contribute to a greater general understanding of this very important public problem.

PUBLIC LECTURES

(Leon Mandel Hall)

I. Monday, July 7, 8:30 P.M.—"What Have the Americas in Common?" HERMINIO PORTELL VILÁ

II. Tuesday, July 8, 4:30 P.M.—"The Strategy of Hemispheric Defense." GEORGE FIELDING ELIOT

III. Wednesday, July 9, 4:30 P.M.—"Inter-American Trade and Financial Problems." EDUARDO VILLASEÑOR

IV. Thursday, July 10, 4:30 P.M.—"Raw Materials and Inter-American Solidarity." ARTHUR R. UPGREN

V. Friday, July 11, 4:30 P.M.—"Canada and Hemispheric Solidarity." FRANK SCOTT

VI. Monday, July 14, 4:30 P.M.—"Cultural Relations among the American Countries." DANIEL SAMPER ORTEGA

VII. Tuesday, July 15, 4:30 P.M.—"Pan-Americanism and the World Order." J. FRED RIPPY

ROUND-TABLE CONFERENCES

(Public Administration Clearing House)

Chairman: WALTER H. C. LAVES

I. Tuesday, July 8, 2:00 P.M.—"The Setting of the Problem and the Impact of World War II upon the Americas." *Leader:* J. FRED RIPPY

PREFACE

II. Tuesday, July 8, 7:30 P.M.—"Barriers to Inter-American Solidarity." *Leader:* ERNESTO MONTENEGRO

III. Wednesday, July 9, 2:00 P.M.—"Military Defense of the Americas." *Leader:* HUGH M. COLE

IV. Wednesday, July 9, 7:30 P.M.—"Capital Investment in Latin America." *Leader:* JACOB VINER

V. Thursday, July 10, 2:00 P.M.—"Raw-Material Resources of the Americas." *Leader:* JOHN C. DE-WILDE

VI. Thursday, July 10, 7:30 P.M.—"Inter-American Industry and Trade." *Leader:* BENJAMIN WALLACE

VII. Friday, July 11, 2:00 P.M.—"Labor Standards in the Americas." *Leader:* DAVID H. BLELLOCH

VIII. Friday, July 11, 7:30 P.M.—"Inter-American Transportation." *Leader:* ROBERT S. PLATT

IX. Monday, July 14, 2:00 P.M.—"Humanitarian Co-operation." *Leader:* ARTHUR SWEETSER

X. Monday, July 14, 7:30 P.M.—"Inter-American Political Relations." *Leader:* QUINCY WRIGHT

XI. Tuesday, July 15, 2:00 P.M.—"Institutions for Inter-American Co-operation." *Leader:* PERCY E. CORBETT

WALTER H. C. LAVES, *Editor*

UNIVERSITY OF CHICAGO
August 1941

TABLE OF CONTENTS

WHAT HAVE THE AMERICAS IN COMMON?

By HERMINIO PORTELL VILÁ

Professor of History of the Americas at the University of Havana, Cuba; sometime Guggenheim Fellow in Cuban American History; Delegate Plenipotentiary of Cuba to the Seventh International Conference of American States (Montevideo, 1933); author of *Historia de Cuba en sus relaciones con los Estados Unidos y España*, etc.

WHAT HAVE THE AMERICAS
IN COMMON?

I CANNOT help feeling that the question assigned to me as the subject of this lecture should be preceded by another question, namely, "Do the Americas really have anything in common?"

There are people who will be ready to assert that the two Americas have nothing in common. These people are less numerous today than they used to be; but we have all known them, and the two Americas have long suffered in their progress and in their understanding of each other as a result of the ideas and the social, economic, and political attitudes of such people. They cannot be identified with any particular country or any given climate; they are found wherever ignorance rules, wherever material values outweigh cultural and moral values, wherever extreme nationalism is rampant. Persons holding this view have been found in all our countries, whether we think of Argentina or the United States, Brazil or Uruguay, Cuba or Chile, Mexico or Colombia, Peru or Haiti.

There are other people who, allowing themselves to be carried away by their enthusiasm, fancy that everything in the two Americas is held in common and that the same characteristics prevailing in North America can be found in South America or are easily transplanted from one region into the other.

There is no question in my mind that these extreme views are fundamentally wrong, but there is still enough evidence to prove conclusively that the two Americas treasure many things in common. Many basic traits can be found in both Anglo-America and Latin America, and many more can be transplanted and extended into practically every country in the New World.

The two Americas include lands with all kinds of climate and with all types of economic activity. There are some agricultural and mining enterprises everywhere, although most of them, or at least the most important ones, are located in limited areas. Shipping concerns are restricted to certain nations and unevenly distributed among them. All the countries import foreign capital, although not in the same proportion. There will not be more than three or four of our republics able to export capital in any appreciable amount, and, compared with the billions of United States investments in Latin America, Argentinian, Cuban, Peruvian, or Mexican surpluses of capital for investment abroad are negligible. Industry, both heavy and light, is predominantly in the hands of the United States. Notwithstanding the fact that Argentina, Brazil, Chile, and, to some extent, Mexico and Cuba now are making notable strides in industrial progress, all of them are still far behind the stage of Belgium, Sweden, or Czechoslovakia in terms of equipment, skilled personnel, and output. If the comparison is made with the United States, Great Britain, Germany, Japan, or even Russia or Italy, the industrial backwardness of the Latin-American nations is astounding. They have raw materials; they have a higher standard of living than some European countries, probably higher than one or two southern or western states of the United States and unquestionably superior to anything found in "darker" Africa, the South Seas (Australia and New Zealand excluded), and Asia. The élite in all Latin-American countries have attained a high cultural level which is comparable to the best in the rest of the world; but in their own countries the élite have failed to provide their peoples with an intelligent, energetic, and well-integrated leadership to bring about the transformation of colonial society into modern nations. The failure of these leading men cannot be excused on grounds of lack of time or opportunities, because most Latin-American countries have had a century or more of independence and there have been many opportunities that have been permitted to pass due to lack of leadership.

Colonial life in Latin America started more than

one hundred years before the founding of James-
town or Plymouth. The Spanish and Portuguese
languages were taught, learned, and spoken by
Europeans, Indians, Negroes, and half-breeds or
mestizos, of the Hispanic-American world, before
Elizabeth of England or Philip of Spain had even
been born. There were printing presses, colleges, li-
braries, anthropological studies, Indian education,
planned economies, etc., in Latin America since
early in the sixteenth century, when the Atlantic
seacoast of North America was almost untouched
by the Europeans. That interesting process of the
"give and take" of civilizations that took place in
the New World between the invaders and the conquered peoples was almost completed in Latin
America before it was started in the Thirteen Colonies, but the latter were able to profit from the mistakes and the successes of both Spain and Portugal
in the founding and development of colonial society. The earlier date of development in Latin
America does not necessarily mean that the process
of colonial evolution was different if compared with
the Thirteen Colonies but rather that the British
had a fine chance to avoid the mistakes of the Spaniards. Fernando Ortiz has just invented a new so-
ciological word to express what was the result of the
"give and take," namely, "transculturation," i.e.,
the transfer from one people to another, and vice
versa, of everything constituting a culture: lan-

guage, knowledge, experience, labor, refinement, energy, convictions, and objectives.

Transculturation being the exchange of cultural values and elements, the effect of the process was determined by the values and elements found in every group of peoples. Taken as a whole, each native group could give only what it had and could receive only what the colonizing country was willing and able to give.

There cannot be any question, therefore, that we have in common in this part of the world a complex cultural heritage in which the European traits were superimposed upon the native elements. The latter were the Indian stocks whose resistance or whose adaptability to Western civilization helped to shape the colonial society and today exert their influence upon the American Southwest, Mexico, Central America, Ecuador, Peru, Bolivia, and Paraguay. Very nearly four hundred thousand inhabitants of the United States are officially classified as Indians, and in Mexico and Peru the Indians number some sixteen and seven millions, respectively. Altogether, there must be thirty million Indians in the two Americas, roughly considered, or 15 per cent of the total population in the New World.

Wherever the Indian has been recognized as entitled to the treatment of a human being for a sufficient time to overcome distrust and non-co-operative habits, his reactions have been promising and his contributions in many fields notable. The social, economic, and cultural redemption of the Indians of the Americas would contribute to the solution of many problems in the countries having Indians, including the United States. No nation can safely live and develop if a part of its population is permanently excluded from responsibilities and advantages on racial grounds. To do this weakens the social body and makes it an easy prey to demagogues who seek the support of disgruntled elements. There cannot be a more useful contribution to national unity and to inter-American solidarity than the suppression of racial discrimination and unwarranted social prejudices.

The New World received Negroes from Africa and also from Spain, Portugal, and even England. The Negro was so well known all over Europe for centuries that the first Negroes brought by the Spaniards to Santo Domingo were Spanish Negroes. From the first arrivals of colored slaves up to 1871, when Cuba received the last shipment of Africans smuggled into the island (the last shipment ever to come across the Atlantic, according to all available evidence), millions of Negroes were sold into slavery in the two Americas. At one time the maroons of Jamaica, who had for years resisted the British, were sent to the northernmost British colonies as a punishment. It can be said that the

WHAT HAVE WE IN COMMON?

Negro was all over the New World, from the Gulf of St. Lawrence down to Patagonia. Although a few countries have been able to absorb the colored elements into the social body—notably Argentina and Uruguay—the Negro population of the two Americas probably aggregates thirty million people. The United States and Brazil alone have some twenty million Negro citizens.

If the European and the Indian contributed some important cultural traits to the civilization of the Americas, the Negro has also left his imprint upon it, and we can detect his influence everywhere. What we have as a result of these mixed influences is a sort of half-breed civilization, a product of a *mestizaje* of races and cultures that has been going on for centuries and that has been taking place even in the countries where they boast of a nonexisting racial purity of the white population. Herskovits has given us recognized scientific evidence to prove that there are very few pure Negroes in the United States, and that is true, too, in the case of the Latin-American republics. We cannot, however, go any further here into the question of racial crossing as a distinctive and common feature of the social body of the two Americas.

Language barriers are fast disappearing in the New World, a situation entirely different from what we can find in Europe, Asia, or Africa, where a multiplicity of languages continues to prevail.

INTER-AMERICAN SOLIDARITY

The peoples of the New World speak English, Spanish, Portuguese, or French, with typical inflections and local words whose influence upon the original languages continues to grow day after day, changing their vocabularies and even their pronunciation. We have a most remarkable case of cultural unity taking shape before our eyes, because the contact areas for each two of these languages are zones where the peoples speak both of them in addition to a sort of emerging lingua franca whose possibilities are boundless. There is a certain tendency to minimize or to hold in contempt the lingua franca of the Americas, but it should be recalled that similar border languages were found as elements in the early history of the proudest languages of today. The free commercial intercourse, the spread of education and modern culture, the increase in traveling, and the contribution of the movies and the radio will accelerate that process, and in due course of time the peoples of the Americas will be able to have a basic vocabulary in each of the four languages of the New World. There will be a new spirit of understanding and collaboration when the language barrier has been reduced to a minimum. This would be a real contribution to the solution of most problems of international co-operation in the Western Hemisphere. It would be unthinkable in Europe, owing to the multiplicity of languages.

WHAT HAVE WE IN COMMON?

The goal is easily within our reach. There are people full of suspicions regarding the spread of the English language into Latin America. They see the marines, the salesmen, and the bankers of ruthless methods speaking English, but they fail to acknowledge or pretend not to consider that that is also the English of John Dewey, Robert Millikan, Sylvanus Morley, Ernest Hemingway, Sinclair Lewis, and of thousands of scientists, philosophers, writers, sociologists, and reformers. Likewise, the Spanish and the Portuguese talked in Latin America are not solely the languages of dictators and disreputable politicians but those of Ricardo Rojas, Afranio Peixoto, Fernando Ortiz, Germán Arciniegas, Antonio Caso, Enrique Juan Palacios, J. Enrique Zanetti, and many men of science and letters. The people of the United States do not have the exact figures regarding the Latin Americans who read and speak and even write the English language, but there are millions south of the Rio Grande who can directly approach American culture without translations into Spanish and Portuguese. This the circulation managers of magazines and papers have long known, and book publishers are just beginning to realize it with their explorations of the neglected Latin-American market for good books. As to the Latin Americans, they also ignore the interest of the new generation in the United States in the languages, the history, and the culture of the other Americans. The recent survey on Latin-American studies in American institutions of higher learning, made by the Division of Intellectual Co-operation of the Pan-American Union, shows that there are 729 professors offering 981 courses to 17,801 students in 383 universities and colleges on the history, the literature, the economic life, the arts, the geography, the education, and the agriculture of Latin America. It is worth noting that these figures exclude courses given in high schools as well as Spanish-language courses in universities and colleges.

A few weeks ago the school system of the city of New York launched a campaign to make its one million children and its forty thousand teachers Pan-American conscious. More than seventy-five Pan-American clubs, with an aggregate membership of some two thousand students, are already in operation in New York City. There is an enrolment of thirty-eight thousand pupils in Spanish, which is second only to French in its total number and larger for the term than the enrolment in all the other foreign and classical languages combined. There has been a substantial increase in the enrolment to learn Portuguese, too. The interest in Spanish and Portuguese is produced not by interest in the European powers once masters of Latin America but by the coming of age of the republics in the other America, growing in population, in economic importance, in military power, and in culture. Theodore Roosevelt, impressed by the formidable impetus back of the same growth, remarked that while the nineteenth century had belonged to the United States, rising to become a world power in little over one hundred years of independence, the twentieth century was the century of the Latin-American republics.

What we have just said regarding the growing interest in Spanish, Portuguese, and Latin-American topics in New York City is also true throughout the rest of the United States, even in the Middle West, long isolated from direct contacts with Latin America. Although in the past there have been fluctuations in inter-American relations, it seems that this time we all mean to establish that permanent good understanding and that knowledge of each other, without prejudice or suspicion, upon which the cultural unity of the New World must be based.

Not many months ago President John A. Mackay of the Union Theological Seminary, speaking in California on Pan-American relations, made the surprising statement that fear was drawing us together, that the countries of Anglo-America and Latin America were becoming conscious of the fact that they have to stand united in order to survive the threats of expansion and world domination from across the seas. Not all of us are prepared to admit that fear is what draws us together, and it is not a healthy sign that this interesting movement of continental solidarity and co-operation should be explained in terms of the common danger. No permanent ties among countries can exist if they are based on fear, because fear is a negative factor in understanding; and to build closer relations upon it is like building upon sandy foundations. For, once fear vanishes, nothing remains but hatred, suspicion, and prejudice. It is undeniable that fear has been and still is one of the leading causes for the unhappy conflict in Europe, and we must escape its effects on this side of the Atlantic.

International co-operation in the Americas has to spring from convictions—deeply felt convictions of a common destiny of progress, equal justice for all, freedom and independence and general welfare. It is of paramount importance to our peoples that we approach each other without fear of aggression from outside or among ourselves. That can be done through international policies proscribing selfishness, demagoguery, and impositions. The principle of responsibility has to be honored both by the big power and by the smaller nation, and, once the people become accustomed to that system, there will be but very few incidents to disturb inter-American relations.

The American republics represent one of the outstanding wonders in the history of civilization.

WHAT HAVE WE IN COMMON?

Little over one hundred and fifty years ago they were the colonial possessions of European powers and they were pitifully underpopulated and more or less backward when compared with their mother-countries. None of them revolted deliberately against a perfect home government. All revolted because of a determination to tolerate political oppression, economic exploitation, and social discrimination no longer. This was true in the Thirteen Colonies, in the Provincias Unidas de la Plata, in the Gran Colombia, in Chile, in Brazil, and in Mexico. Half a century was enough for most of them to challenge metropolitan domination, winning their wars of independence and doubling the number of sovereign states of the world in the period from Bunker Hill to Ayacucho. Each country achieved independence with the social, economic, and political equipment that it had had for centuries. It happened that the equipment of the United States, reflecting the advantages that the colonists had enjoyed as a consequence of British political maturity as well as of the struggle between the kings and parliament, was better balanced and more advanced. On the other hand, the colonial system of Spain had aimed to digest into a single social body all the different ethnic elements in her colonies and to maintain a highly centralized control over them, so as to embrace all the activities, even the most elementary activities of the colonists, under a strict despotism. It is no wonder, therefore, that Latin-American colonial society has had such a painful and slow evolution, running into difficulties not yet completely conquered. Royal supremacy in Spain was not tempered by a Magna Carta and after the War of the Comunidades, in the time of Charles V, was not challenged anew until the very epoch when Latin Americans were revolting for independence in the last century. Recent elements prevailing in Spain try to prove that absolutism was imported into that country by the French dynasty in the eighteenth century, but the truth is that the traditional political institutions of Spain, both in the Cortes and in the municipal *fueros*, were abolished by the Hapsburgs, that is to say, by Charles V, founder of the German dynasty in Spain, who put an end to local liberties among the Spaniards. His successors—the kings of the Austrian family and, later on, the Bourbon princes—did not want to grant their subjects in the colonies the rights they had denied to their metropolitan subjects, and therefore Latin America did not have a chance to be trained in political life.

The historical unity of the New World is a fact attested by all events in the evolution of the two Americas, notwithstanding temporary setbacks and apparent denials, some of which we have pointed out in the preceding paragraphs. But there is more to be noted that we also have in common.

WHAT HAVE WE IN COMMON?

We live in a world of liberty in this hemisphere, and the Americas, together with Great Britain, have more than once been the last and safest refuge of freedom and independence. Weak and underpopulated as the United States was during the Napoleonic Wars and their aftermath, and in spite of the natural turbulence of the War of Independence in Hispanic America, it was in these continents that political refugees from Europe found a safe haven, and it was our climate of liberty that attracted them to us. The Americas certainly were the lands of opportunity in an economic sense, and that was a great inducement; but they also were, above all, free countries where personal effort, civic pride, intellectual merit, and social contributions were rewarded. In Europe they tried to set back the clock of human progress to put the world where it had been before the French Revolution, with privilege, injustice, arbitrary government, obscurantism, and prejudice vainly trying to uproot the new ideas and to change citizens into serfs anew. They called that the period of the Holy Alliance, but it really should be called the period of the Reactionary International, never openly acknowledged but as much of a fact as the Socialist International of later years. The Americas offered their climate of liberty and the protection of their free institutions to the victims of the Reactionary International set up at the Congress of Vienna, and they continued to do so and are still doing so. The failure of the July revolution of 1830 in Poland and Italy, as well as the disaster of the European liberal movement of 1848, threw upon our shores men like Garibaldi, Avezzana, Kossuth, Schurz, and thousands of others, in the same way that modern reaction brings us Einstein, Mann, De los Ríos, Ortega y Gasset, Giralt, Maurois, Sforza, Borgese, and numerous other victims of the totalitarian regimes of the Right and of the Left. Although democracy is far from perfect in the Latin-American republics as a whole, they associate themselves with the United States to receive and to honor outstanding men fleeing from persecution at home and anxious to find countries of freedom and tolerance.

That trait of attracting the liberal, the nonconformist, and the progressive elements from other parts of the world and of providing them with the social, economic, and political conditions they were longing for is a part of the American tradition which we all cherish and which draws the peoples of the Americas to the side of democracy and freedom.

There will be cynical observers who will point out that there are dictatorships in Latin America and that in some countries the state of dictatorship seems to be chronic and permanent. There is no reason to deny that fact, but at the same time it does not destroy the truth of the main assertion re-

garding popular sympathy for democracy and freedom, because at bottom there is a century-old
struggle in Latin America to establish democratic
institutions. That is the real cause for what has
been called the "revolutionary habit" among Latin
Americans. The "poll tax" and its abuses, the one-
party system of the South, and the virtual dis-
franchisement of the southern Negroes in the
United States are similarly proof not of the non-
democratic character of the United States but of
local conflicts for political domination based upon
economic or racial pretexts that sooner or later will
be solved by suppressing discrimination and injustice, as is the will of a large majority among the
Americans.

Democracy is a perfect state, and perfection cannot be attained overnight. England has been aiming at it for some seven centuries and has not yet
reached the happy stage of spotless democracy;
the other big European powers have plunged into
despotism of the worst type, modernly called the
totalitarian system. It is very natural that the
young countries of the New World struggle with
the realization of democracy; but they do not re-
nounce it or give up their faith. On the contrary,
all of them treasure in common the democratic
ideal, so simply expressed by Bentham, of "the
greatest good for the greatest number," a political
and social regime in which "every man ought to

count for one and none for more than one." The dictators of totalitarian countries will discredit these principles and refuse to abide by them; in the New World, on the contrary, not even the most unscrupulous dictator will make a statement against democracy, even while he betrays it. It is democracy, freedom, equal opportunity, justice, lack of prejudice, and real tolerance that are the very soul of the peoples of the Americas, the ideals they cherish in common and hope to have realized. The Latin-American dictator, at his worst, will always consider his regime a temporary one and will attempt to justify it on the ground that his country needs it in order to have democracy later on.

As a matter of fact, if democracy results in "the greatest good for the greatest number," the New World is the ideal place to attain that result. The vastness of these continents, where there are three countries bigger than Europe and many others of considerable size, must necessarily prevent conflicts of imperialistic expansion of the type caused today by the so-called *Lebensraum* ambitions of the Germans. Oil, coal, vital minerals of all classes, are to be found everywhere in the two Americas. With very few exceptions, all the plants of the world can be grown in a continent having all kinds of climate. What we have been able to do with human races and cultures mixing on this side of the Atlantic we are also doing with foreign trees, vegetables, and grasses, crossing them with native species according to that universal rule of transculturation common to everything in the New World. The only limitations to industrialization extending throughout the two Americas are to be found in the capital, raw materials, fuel, and technical knowledge needed. Even these requisites are easily found and in certain countries are being co-ordinated with great success, notably in Argentina, Brazil, and Chile, in addition to the United States and Canada.

A great industrial output, however, presupposes an important domestic market to consume a large portion of it and to act as a pivot and a balance in the international market. A superficial observer will say that there are great differences of population and consumption between the two Americas, but it would be a mistake to make too broad generalizations in support of this point. The tendency to improve the standard of living is general everywhere, and there are certain areas of Latin America where the standard of living is higher than it is in large sections of the South and the Southwest of the United States, with the corresponding high consumption of domestic goods. Economic self-sufficiency, the goal of the modern state, with all its dangers and its benefits that the United States knows so well, attracts the Latin Americans too. Unless there is a rapid and well-planned remedy for it, we shall before long see the trend to economic autarchy gaining momentum in Latin America.

The growth of the population of the New World

is another important factor that must be considered as common to all the republics. The late Professor Raymond Pearl left us some startling data on the subject in an article printed in the *Yale Review*. Professor Pearl made an analysis of the available figures for the growth of the population in some of the nations of the world and listed the twenty fastest-growing countries, thirteen of which were American republics, the United States included. Brazil, adding very nearly two million people a year, topped the list, with Cuba in second place, and Uruguay, the Dominican Republic, Argentina, Bolivia, Peru, Costa Rica, Salvador, Nicaragua, the United States, Mexico, and Chile following them in that order. The aggregate populations of the Latin-American nations reach one hundred and twenty-two million people. Brazil has well over forty-five million people, and a few years of peace have given Mexico a population of twenty millions, while Argentina is close to fourteen millions. In one or two more generations we shall see some of these republics playing roles among the leading powers of the world in proportion to the size, resources, culture, and progress now being developed at a tremendous speed.

It would be a great mistake for the two Americas to ignore any longer their common destiny and not to develop a permanent system of continental solidarity and general understanding that will work in any circumstances. We have at our disposal the means to prevent the New World from becoming another Europe, divided by rivalries of power and domination. History shows us that, save for a few unimportant and temporary conflicts, we have been at peace for long periods, that we participate in each other's difficulties and successes, and that the safety, the prosperity, the peace, the progress, and the happiness of the peoples of the New World are one inseparable concern of all. The first real contact of the United States with Gran Colombia, revolted under Miranda, when Bolívar was practically unknown, was an appropriation of money, by act of the Congress of the United States, to relieve the suffering of the victims of the dreadful earthquake of March 26, 1812, that destroyed the city of Caracas, Venezuela. That highly significant fact of good neighborliness has been repeated more than one hundred times in the intervening years as a proof that we are not alone in our sorrows and our happiness as members of the international community of American states. Geography teaches us that there is an isolation of this New World, surrounded by oceans and making communications among our countries more and more regular and fruitful. There are continuous lands, seas, and air that are American and common to the Americas. Recent inter-American agreements have implemented this geographical fact, with the Declaration of Havana of 1940 calling for an all-American policy against aggression and setting our belief in rights and decency against the totalitarian doctrine of might and violence. In the economic field there is not a single legitimate and sound national interest that cannot be conciliated in a well-planned interchange with those of the other countries; and, when the conciliation demands a sacrifice here or there, it must be borne as a contribution to the common good and to the cause of continental solidarity. Selfish minorities and prejudiced groups of the two Americas, putting their petty passions ahead of the great aims of understanding and cooperation among the countries of the New World, do not exemplify American ideals but, on the contrary, are helping the totalitarians to break the unity of purpose of our democracies and as such are not entitled to the benefits of our political and economic systems, whose correlative duties they refuse to fulfil.

We cannot realize our destinies as individual nations and as American republics if the totalitarian doctrine becomes the rule of international life. We have fought for freedom; we want to abolish intolerance and prejudice and to suppress privilege. We also strive for a civilization that will develop around justice and democratic progress. What we have built up around these principles may or may not be the realization of what the founders of our republics wanted us to have, and there will be different degrees in our republican success; but whatever it may be, it is unquestionably superior to what we have had before as well as to what we might have in a totalitarian world. It is not only in the past and in the present that we have our common history, populations, institutions, progress, and ideals worth saving and fighting for but also in the future—a future that is the result of the work and the faith of many generations whose legacy of an American civilization based upon democracy we cannot betray if we are to be the worthy descendants of Jefferson and Lincoln, of Bolívar and San Martín, of Juárez and Martí. Our Martí, the last of the American liberators, left us these words, written here in the United States during the last century, when he was in contact with your Walt Whitman:

Heroes are those fighting to give freedom to peoples or suffering in poverty and misfortune to defend the great truth. But those who fought for ambition, who want to enslave other peoples, to increase their power or to deprive other men of their lands, they are no heroes in spite of military success: they are international criminals. . . . . The world has just two fields: one for those hating liberty, and one for those who love it. . . . . All men loving justice and right will fight for liberty wherever it is in danger and by doing so, they will be fighting for their dignity as men. . . . . .

The words of Martí apply to present-day conditions in a world torn from its natural evolution by the forces of evil, now expanding the domains of intolerance, injustice, and despotism and threatening our inheritance of democracy—the one we received in common more than a century ago and have been developing in common ever since, with the vicissitudes of human effort. In the same way, in common, we must defend that democracy at the price of any sacrifice and through the finest example of international solidarity that the world has yet seen: the solidarity of the American peoples.

THE STRATEGY OF HEMISPHERIC DEFENSE

By GEORGE FIELDING ELIOT
Military Critic, formerly Major, Military Intelligence
Reserve, U.S. Army

THE STRATEGY OF HEMISPHERIC DEFENSE

I THINK it is becoming clear that the word "defense" has had a very bad effect on American popular thinking on the subject of the military policy of our country. We see now, going up and down the land, many gentlemen who insist on the strictest possible construction of the word "defense." They seem distressed at the thought that any American soldier, sailor, or marine should ever be asked to leave our shores.

In effect, in face of the terrible increase in range, in speed, and in the destructive power of modern weapons of war, these advocates of defense pure and simple desire that this republic, if fight it must, shall fight on its own soil with its battle-fields lighted by the flames of its own blazing cities.

The view of what may be called "military circles," so frequently referred to in an anonymous fashion, is something quite other than this. A military man sees defense in an entirely different aspect. He does not desire to sit upon the shores of this nation and await the initiative of whatever foe we may have. He hopes, by being strong enough, to avoid having to fight at all because he knows from experience that war is a very terrible thing, and he has no desire that this nation should take part in it.

He knows also, however, that there is no assurance that we shall never have to fight again, and he knows full well that if we do fight, under modern conditions especially, it will be far better that the fighting should take place elsewhere than within our own territory.

The basic consideration, therefore, in the defense of the Americas—the defense of this country or of the Americas as a whole—is a military policy so designed that, if war should come to us, should be forced upon us, or if the making of war should seem to be a necessary instrument of national policy, we shall be able to make war somewhere else than here—that the battlefields upon which we fight, if they must be lighted by the flames of blazing cities, shall be lighted by the flames of the enemy's cities rather than our own.

There is really no such thing in modern war as pure defense. It is conceivable that a force on the battlefield or a nation in the larger field of military policy might stand on the absolutely static defensive, doing absolutely nothing except to repel such assaults as might be directed against it. This is a policy which has nothing to recommend it from experience, however. It has never been successful. It seems very unlikely that it ever will be successful.

Translated into the field of national policy, we have seen again and again where the defensive idea has dominated both in the military sense and in the wider political sphere. We have seen nation after nation go down before the offensive power of those who have chosen to make the sword the instrument of their ambitions.

Clausewitz tells us that defense is the strongest form of war, but he hastens to add that nothing can be accomplished by it because it has a negative object; it is the stronger form of war only in the sense that it enables comparatively small forces to hold positions for a time against assault under circumstances when these forces themselves could not take the offensive.

But it accomplishes nothing more than the holding of a position or, again, in the political sense, perhaps the delay imposed for a brief time on the ambitions of a neighbor-state. It accomplishes nothing positive.

Sometimes it is necessary for a small state to adopt a defensive attitude because it has no means of doing anything else. In that case its hope, as against the aggression of a great state, is merely to make it cost them too dearly to undertake an attack upon it. Switzerland is in this position. Switzerland knows that Germany can take it over, but it hopes that its terrain and its excellently co-ordinated military system of defense will make it so costly that the Germans will prefer not to.

A great state cannot pursue such a policy. A great state has a positive policy of its own. It has its prestige to think of; it has almost daily contacts with those states with whom its policy is in conflict. Its leaders realize that force underlies all diplomacy as a possible final arbiter and that, while diplomats do not talk of these unpleasant things in their day-to-day exchanges, it realizes, as Grover Cleveland told us, that a state which is unable to maintain its policies by force in the last analysis is subject to continual insults, to paying continually the price of its weakness in its inability to obtain its end or to protect its interests and those of its citizens.

The state which occupies an insular position, such as the United States, is in a peculiarly admirable position to protect its interests and to maintain its rights, provided it possesses the command of the sea; but here again its policy must be based on the nature of the military instruments which enforce that policy, which lie behind it, and in naval warfare particularly by the very mobile nature of the instruments which it uses—fleets and aircraft. A defensive in the pure sense of the word is the worst possible policy for such a force to adopt. A fleet which supinely awaits the attack of the enemy, as did the Russian fleet in the Russo-Japanese War, for example, accomplishes nothing.

HEMISPHERIC DEFENSE

In all defense, properly so called, there is the element of the offensive, just as in all offense there is the element of the defensive. The separation between them can never be sharp and clear. Just as there is such a thing as a purely static defense, there is also such a thing as an absolutely all-out, headlong offensive which takes no account of anything except the desire to get at the enemy and destroy him. That has, on occasion, worked; but against a properly handled, properly disciplined force it has just as little chance of success as the static defense.

When the Persians attacked the Greeks at Marathon, the Greeks had an excellent defensive formation. They were able to beat off the attacks of the Persians, but they were not able to destroy the Persian army because they had not yet developed the phalanx into that instrument of defensive and offensive warfare which Philip and Alexander later developed. When the phalanx had added to it the striking wings of cavalry and lightly armed infantry, it became so formidable that it overthrew a Persian empire.

Against the headlong rush of the brave but ill-disciplined Gauls, the Roman legions afforded a somewhat more flexible device. They added to the disciplined base of armored infantry, which the phalanx provided, the addition of fire power, missile weapons, the javelins of the Roman infantry, and provided a flexible organization which enabled the enemy, when he had struck and been held by the troops at the front, to be struck in the flank by other detachments, whether infantry or cavalry. This was a very considerable improvement on the phalanx because it enabled operations to be conducted over broken ground and under almost all circumstances likely to be encountered on the battlefield.

You observe that in all these ancient battles the principle held fast that there was an element of defensive in the offense and one of offensive in the defense, for the phalanx always afforded a solid rock on which the offensive elements—cavalry and lightly armed infantry—could fall back if they were beaten, just as the flexibility and missile power of the Roman legion and its organization into cohorts, some of which would be held in reserve, afforded the first appearance of a true reserve on the battlefield and enabled advantage to be taken of the turn of events whether favorable or unfavorable.

Today we consider the most important principles of war to be those of concentration, offensive action, and security. Concentration is the use of all your means for the accomplishment of your principal end, holding out nothing that is not absolutely necessary elsewhere. Offensive action means the use of this concentrated power to achieve your end, instead of sitting still and waiting to see what the enemy is going to do. Security implies that, while you are doing all this, you do not expose any vital interests of your own to the enemy's attack.

All these must be kept in mind. A general who, while undertaking offensive action, neglects the security of his base or of some center or element vital either to his own operations or to the welfare or morale of his country is liable to suffer a very severe shock at the hands of an enterprising enemy.

On the other hand, a general who is so concerned with security that he is unable, because of his assignment to security missions of the greater part of his forces, to take the offensive is not going to accomplish anything, and in the end he will be beaten because, as Frederick the Great said, you cannot be strong everywhere. Sooner or later, if you attempt to defend everything, an enterprising enemy will search out and find your weak spots and strike at them as the Germans struck at the French weak spot on the Meuse in the spring of last year.

Indeed, I think the Maginot Line itself, and the conception which lay behind it, has taken far too great a grip on the American mind. We hear of our Maginot Line being the middle of the Atlantic Ocean, along a string of outposts which we have established there. One would suppose that this string of outposts was a row of forts intended to impose an impregnable barrier to the advance of any force across the Atlantic Ocean.

Nothing of the sort! These outposts are points of support for the operation of mobile air and naval forces whose missions are entirely offensive. We hear of the attempt to distinguish between offensive and defensive weapons—such an attempt as Mr. Hoover made at the last general disarmament conference—when, as a matter of fact, there is no such distinction.

I was once asked to show how an antiaircraft gun could possibly be an offensive weapon, and yet it is well recognized that all offensive action must proceed from a defended base, from a secure base. The gun which makes the base secure, from which a bombardment airplane proceeds upon its mission, is just as much a part of the offensive mission of that bombardment airplane as the plane itself and just as necessary a part of the system which makes offensive action by that plane possible.

In the same battle it may be necessary, and usually is, to take the defensive on one part of the field, pinning down a certain part of the enemy's force, in order to concentrate your main effort for the offensive elsewhere. Every commander who is forced to assume the general defensive as his attitude hopes to pass from the defensive to the offensive later.

You may ask how this can be, if he is so weak

that he has to take the defensive to begin with. He hopes that the enemy, by injudicious attack, will expose himself to a counterblow or he hopes that he will be able so to reduce the enemy's forces by the attrition of battle that an opportunity will be afforded him later or he hopes to receive reinforcements. He takes the defensive to await their arrival.

The defensive and the offensive are indeed instruments in the hands of a skilled commander, and their judicious employment, one with the other, comprises a great part of what is called the art of war.

Today we are seeing again exemplified the truth that even in defense, assumed as an attitude for the time being, the heart and soul of the success of defense is counterattack. It has been the Russian armored counterattack which has been the chief element in slowing down the German advance so far. On the question as to whether those counterattacks can be kept up must turn, for the moment, at any rate, any speculation as to the future of German attack upon Russia.

As a matter of the policy of states, these questions of offense and defense are of the greatest importance. We have considered the question of a small state like Switzerland, which does not have the means to take the offensive against its great neighbors as compared with the policy of a great state like our own. We are coming more and more to a realization of the responsibility that lies upon us in a world which is shrinking so rapidly in size, as a practical matter, that we can no longer shrug off as of no importance the occurrences in Europe, Asia, and Africa.

We have, in fact, become the greatest of the great powers. We have, by a strange development of circumstances which few could have foreseen in the early days of this republic, become for the next hundred years or so, at any rate, the greatest of the sea powers. It will no longer be possible for the British people to maintain in their islands (which have lost their insular security by reason of the development of the airplane) the bases and the industrial strength necessary for the maintenance of vast fleets.

The secure base and the secure industrial support which sea power demands must now be removed to the continent of North America—perhaps in part to that of Australia as industry develops there. It is in the control of the sea, to begin with, that our security rests; but we cannot develop this control any longer on the basis of an imaginary Maginot Line drawn halfway down the middle of the Atlantic Ocean and of the Pacific Ocean.

In other words, the strategy of hemispheric defense is a strategy of the command of the sea, and by that I mean the command of the sea in the sense that the British Commonwealth of Nations has for the last two hundred years had command of the sea. In my judgment there is no other, no lesser, policy which will serve our ends. There is no lesser policy which will assure a defeat of those who are now striving to overthrow our civilization by force of arms and have set out upon the conquest of the world. There is no lesser policy which, when that defeat has been accomplished, will enable the peace and order of the world to be maintained during the period of reconstruction and readjustment which must follow upon military victory.

For make no mistake about it, if Germany is beaten, it will be because the United States and the British Commonwealth of Nations have jointly created such instruments of military and political and economic control and co-ordination as shall enable them to bring all their resources to bear for that purpose, and this will be based almost wholly upon the command of the sea which joins the various parts of their widely scattered holdings and living-places together. And those instruments will exist when the war is over, and they will be, for a time at any rate, the only means of maintaining any sort of international order.

The defense of the Americas, the defense of those things which make life worth the living for American peoples, North and South, is a matter, first of all, of the defeat of those who would destroy those things and, second, of the rebuilding of a society in which those things can continue to exist.

In both these cases the application of force, of a very large measure of force, is an absolute essential. We cannot accomplish the defense of the Americas by creating a system of bases and forts and threatening to shoot at any rascal who attempts to come within a certain line or across a certain parallel or meridian with the intent to disturb our peace. We can assure the peace only by dealing as drastically as may be necessary with the disturber of the peace and, having dealt with him, by taking such measures as shall see to it that further disturbers either do not arise or are unable to accomplish their object.

Only yesterday all this was brought forcefully home to us by the necessity under which our government found itself compelled to occupy the peaceful distant island of Iceland. It is no longer safe, it is no longer in the military sense possible, for us to assure our security by sitting here at home and talking about defense. The only worthwhile defense, Admiral Farragut once said, is a well-directed fire from your own guns. Applied to the international scene, this means that the risk to be imposed upon a would-be disturber of the world peace must be more than that his attempt may fail; it must be a direct and an immediate risk to his own vital interests, and it means that those who are concerned with the preservation of the peace must possess the means to threaten the vital interests of any would-be aggressor. When such an aggressor is actually in the field, it is a question not of each nation standing in turn upon its defense but of those who are determined to preserve the peace and to have a peaceful, decent world in which to live joining together and using all their means to destroy the aggressor while there is a chance of such joint action being effective, instead of standing, one by one, on the defense and being, one by one, destroyed, each in his own turn and at the aggressor's chosen time in his chosen way.

We cannot undertake a policy, however, of command of the sea as the basis of our military policy on any restricted geographical scale. We cannot, for example, ignore any of the vitally important maritime bottlenecks and crossroads of the world. We have seen in recent months—and I need not here go into detail on the subject—how vitally important is Singapore to the defense of our interests in the Far East and how vitally important, in turn, it is to the maintenance of the British position in the Indian Ocean and to their operations in the Middle East.

I do not think it is quite as well understood how important the so-called strategical arch of the British Empire in Egypt, Palestine, Iraq, and that general region is to our defense, but it is necessary only to glance at a map to observe that there are two routes into the South Atlantic Ocean. It is necessary only to recall that it is the southern part of South America in which Germany is particularly interested because of climatic conditions and that a Germany in control of the Suez Canal, the Mediterranean Sea, and the Red Sea would be able to penetrate into the South Atlantic Ocean around the Cape of Good Hope by a route which we should have singular difficulty in interrupting.

It is not only by Dakar that the threat comes. Unless we had strong bases in the South Atlantic, unless we were prepared to deal with that threat as far away as Mauritius or Madagascar—which we certainly are not—we should have great difficulty in dealing with an Axis thrust into the South Atlantic from that direction.

I mention this merely to show that, with the development of modern warships with their vastly increased cruising ranges and the development, hand in hand with the warship, of the airplane as an instrument of sea power (I have no patience with people who talk about the difference between sea power and air power. There is no dividing-line. The airplane is as much an instrument of sea warfare as of land warfare!), the world has grown so small that he whose safety depends on the command of the sea must be prepared to deal with threats to his control of the sea wherever those threats may arise, must be prepared, to paraphrase the words of Lord Nelson, who, when asked where were the sea frontiers of Britain, replied, "The sea frontiers of Britain are the shore lines of Britain's enemies."

The only policy we can have today that is a successful policy of hemispheric defense is a sea-power policy based on the continent of North America and co-operating with the sea power of the British Commonwealth of Nations, for between us we control every single important maritime point of control in all the world.

This is not a policy of policing the world, as we are sometimes told by those who are terrified by the changes that have been brought about and do not quite see the way to deal with them. It is the old, historic policy of the balance of power.

Now, according to some of our worthy statesmen of today, the balance of power is something that was invented by the European nations in order to justify their innate and evil desires to go to war with each other. As a matter of fact, it is one of the oldest laws governing human and international conduct in the world. It is based on the law of self-preservation, and that stark fact is what we are face to face with right now—the question of self-preservation, of preserving our way of life or being compelled to live according to a way of life which most of us would rather be dead than endure.

During the nineteenth century the sea power of

Great Britain occupied the central position in the European balance of power. There were no great powers outside of Europe. The United States was just becoming one—had not become one yet in the international sense. Britain threw the weight of her sea power one way or the other—and of financial and commercial power which that sea power created and protected with a view to preventing any single Continental nation's becoming supreme on the Continent. She pursued this policy successfully for just under a hundred years after the Battle of Waterloo for the excellent reasons, first, that she had a secure base which could not be invaded by any means then possessed by any Continental power; second, that none of them were able to challenge her at sea; and, third, that they had had a demonstration during the Napoleonic Wars of what sea power could do and of its increasing importance in the economic and industrial world of the dawning machine age.

That importance is increasing daily. It directs itself particularly and very dramatically at this time to the question of armament, which is so completely dependent on industrial support and which demands so continuous a flow of raw materials of increasing quantity and variety coming in great part by sea from distant parts of the world.

No nation is self-sufficient in this respect. The United States is more so than any other, but he

who controls the sea may to a very great extent
control the flow of international commerce and the
flow of the life-blood of armament.

The control of the sea is indeed a very great
power, but again it must be emphasized that it
must be a complete control. This does not mean
policing the world, but it means that a sea power
erected by the common interests of the English-
speaking peoples of the world and based on the
continent of North America can occupy very much
the same position with regard to a world balance of
power, however composed, as the British sea power
based on the island of Great Britain with regard
to the European balance of power during the hundred years of the *pax Britannica*.

The application of these principles by the British
resulted not in the prevention of war but in the
limitation in duration and extent of such wars as
took place. It prevented wars from spreading, from
becoming a really great menace to the world economy. It purchased a hundred years of the greatest
progress that the world has ever seen—this not because the British were nobler or more moral people
than anybody else but because they were a trading
nation and wanted a peaceful world in which they
could trade peacefully.

In pursuing their own interests, they did the
world a great service. In pursuing our own interests, as we always should, we may well be able to do

the world as great a service for the next fifty or one hundred years. But we cannot do it unless we realize that defense—the defense of this hemisphere, the defense of American interests everywhere, the defense of the freedom of our sister-republics to the south of us, the defense of everything that free men everywhere hold dear—is not a matter of standing still and waiting for the enemies of freedom to strike but a matter, rather, of dealing them such blows while opportunity offers as shall make them glad to give up their attempts to destroy freedom.

We do have such an opportunity now. Only yesterday Britain fought alone against Germany. Today Germany is fighting both Britain and the Soviet Union. Tomorrow it is to be hoped that a formidable coalition indeed may be in the field against the ambitions, to use Mr. Churchill's words, of that evil man who would destroy all that Western civilization has built and holds dear.

If the American people have the clear, historical vision which their forefathers seemed to have and arise to that sense of responsibility in a world in which they are just becoming accustomed to the position and responsibilities of a great power, then there will be a defense of the Americas, a defense of freedom, which will be effective, which will accomplish its object, and which will see to it that government of the people, by the people, and for the people shall not perish from the earth.

But this will never be done so long as we listen to those who speak to us in terror of the undertaking of responsibilities outside our continent, of those who are frightened at a distant war but would be willing, apparently, to undertake a war at home— those who tell us that no American fighting man must leave these shores, who apparently consider that American fighting men have the mission solely of fighting after the enemy has been permitted to arrive where he can do damage directly to this country.

This is a false philosophy of defense. It is a philosophy which has proved the ruin of every people who have made it their own. It is a philosophy which, it is to be hoped, the American people now, once and for all, will decisively reject in favor of a new, forward, hopeful, and intelligent policy of using their great strength to protect and defend those things which make America, where those things are threatened.

There is not much time; modern war moves very rapidly. Changes can be brought about from one day to another. We have all seen and understand it. We have an opportunity now, while the Germans are engaged with an enemy which it is clear they underestimated, to take such steps as shall bring the German high command the terrible and sometimes insoluble problems of a two-front war which they were not able to solve last time and which they may not be able to solve this time.

If we are such fools as to sit idly by and allow the Germans to destroy the Russians—and that has no bearing whatever on what we may think of the Russians—and then with Russian resources to turn in full force upon the Western world at last, we shall deserve the fate of fools and that fate will assuredly be ours.

For my own part, having a considerable faith in the last analysis in good, hard, American common sense, I do not believe that we are going either to be fools or to suffer the fate thereof.

INTER-AMERICAN TRADE AND FINANCIAL PROBLEMS

By Eduardo Villaseñor
Director-General del Banco de México
Mexico City

INTER-AMERICAN TRADE AND
FINANCIAL PROBLEMS

I

IF WE set ourselves to search for the origin of the principle of diminishing returns, we shall find that it dates back to the late eighteenth century, when Turgot stated clearly in his *Observations sur la mémoire de M. de St.-Péravy*, published in 1768, that every increase in cultivation would yield less produce and that there was a point of maximum returns per unit of capital applied to a given piece of land. Beyond this point, and before it, there would be smaller returns per unit of capital employed.

At the beginning of the nineteenth century, chiefly as a result of the Napoleonic Wars, British farmers were securing good prices for their produce. But Napoleon's fall gave new impetus to the agitation of landed interests which sought a re-establishment of the corn laws system on a basis that would offer protection to British farmers during the post-war period. Politicians and economists engaged in this controversy, which brought about the protectionist measures of 1815, with their subsequent amendments which were the cause, a quarter of a century later, of a great struggle between protection and free trade. Among those who participated in this controversy, we naturally find Malthus, Ricardo, and Sir Edward West, whose important contribution contains a discussion and statement of this question of diminishing returns.

Malthus, in his *Observations on the Effects of the Corn Laws* (1814), emphasized "the necessity of yearly cultivating and improving more poor land to provide for the demands of an increasing population; which land must, of course, require more labour and dressing and expense of all kinds in its cultivation."

Committees were appointed in both houses of parliament to obtain data and material which would confirm Malthus' views. When Sir Edward West read the reports of these committees, he published a pamphlet (1815) in which he laid down a principle of political economy which had occurred to him, he wrote, some time before:

The principle is simply this, that in the progress of the improvement of cultivation, the raising of rude produce becomes progressively more expensive, or, in other words, the ratio of the net produce of land to its gross produce is continually diminishing.[1]

Ricardo believed that, as population increased, the poorer lands would come under cultivation and

---

[1] *Essay on the Application of Capital to Land: with Observations Showing the Impolicy of Any Great Restriction on the Importation of Corn, and That the Bounty of 1688 Did Not Lower the Price of It*, pp. 1, 2.

the richer lands would be employed more inten-sively, from which he concluded that *the returns per unit of capital and labor applied to land would fall off*. Many other eminent economists dealt with this subject. Finally, many years later, Wicksteed pointed out that the question to be discussed in the principle of diminishing returns was not so much the idea of the fall in returns as that of the limita-tion or *restricted growth* of other factors, a point not mentioned explicitly before. Clearly, he says, if other factors had increased also, no one would have talked of diminishing returns. As he so aptly puts it, "If you double the pastry without doubling the apples, you do not double the pie."

Wicksteed, like Turgot, considers the problem as one of proportionality. Contemporary writers ap-ply this idea not only to the question of the propor-tions in which capital, land, and labor are combined in the process of production but also to problems such as the size of the industrial plant and the scale of the business enterprise.

Thus far, we have roughly outlined the origin, development, and scope of the principle of dimin-ishing returns, which today is part and parcel of contemporary economic theory. Now, it would not seem farfetched to apply this idea of the proportions in which a firm combines its several factors to the economic life of a nation as a whole at any given stage. If in the course of a country's economic development there is a time when most or all of its natural resources have been tapped, and its population has become stationary (because it has ceased growing or because immigration has been suspended), and, on the other hand, owing to the nature of its foreign trade or its internal economic structure, capital continues to accumulate, one may infer that at that stage the proportionality between the factors of production ceases to apply or is about to cease applying to the economic growth of that country, since one of the factors of production—capital—has increased at a far quicker rate than the other factors. For a country to find itself in this position, capital must have been invested successively in those enterprises in which either realized profits or the expectation of profits were greatest, until practically all enterprises were fully supplied with it and some surplus capital remained idle, that is to say, not employed in any form of production at a given moment in the economic life of the country.

The attainment of this particular stage of development calls for several remarks. In the first place, from the domestic point of view, there is a large accumulation of profits which finds no opportunity for profitable reinvestment within the country. Second, from the standpoint of foreign trade, the country probably enjoys a net credit in its balance of payments which reinforces the accumulation of capital.

This accumulation of idle capital probably causes a fall in interest rates. Such a fall might lead some entrepreneurs to carry out previously discarded plans which were then considered "next best" but which may now be expected to yield sufficient gain to allow them a net profit after deducting capital charges at the new low rates of interest.

Competition between investors who wish to participate in the earnings of certain enterprises which still make large profits will result in shares of those enterprises being quoted at a premium, so that the yield on that type of investment will also fall. We then find the country reaching a point of saturation from which it can escape either by having recourse to war (a waste of productive equipment) or to investment abroad (a means of rendering productive some part of its accumulation of idle savings).

This picture is not very different from that painted by classical economists. Adam Smith, for example, says:

> As capitals increase in any country, the profits which can be made by employing them necessarily diminish. . . . . The demand for productive labour . . . . grows every day greater and greater [and] competition raises the wages of labour, and sinks the profits of stock.[2]

Ricardo, moreover, states: "The natural tendency of profits is to fall; for in the progress of society and wealth the additional quantity of food

[2] *Wealth of Nations*, Book II, chap. iv.

required is obtained by the sacrifice of more and more labour."[3] John Stuart Mill expressed similar views some years later when he said: "The rate of profits tends to fall from . . . . an increase of capital beyond population, producing increased competition for labour."[4]

In discussing the factors which counteract the tendency of profits to fall, Mill makes this striking statement concerning the export of capital or, as he calls it, the "perpetual flow of capital into colonies or foreign countries, to seek higher profits than they can obtain at home": "I believe this to have been for many years one of the principal causes by which the decline of profits in England has been arrested."[5] And, further on, he says:

As long as there are old countries where capital increases very rapidly, and new countries where profit is still high, profits in the old countries will not sink to the rate which would put a stop to accumulation; the fall is stopped at the point which sends capital abroad.[6]

This process of capital accumulation which leads to a fall in the rate of profit has also been dealt with by Marx in Volume III of *Das Kapital*. He states that the rate of profit tends to diminish, and he explains this as a function of the increase in the amount of constant capital as compared with vari-

[3] *Principles*, chapter on "Profits."

[4] *Essays on Some Unsettled Questions in Political Economy.*

[5] *Principles* (Ashley's ed.), p. 738.   [6] *Ibid.*, p. 739.

able capital. After a few examples in which he assumes different amounts of constant capital, given the same surplus value, he says:

> In this way, the same rate of surplus-value, with the same degree of labour exploitation, would express itself *in a falling rate of profit*, because the material growth of the constant capital, and consequently of the total capital, implies their growth in value, although not in the same proportion.
>
> If it is furthermore assumed that this gradual change in the composition of capital is not confined to some individual spheres of production, but occurs more or less in all, or at least in the most important ones, so that they imply changes in the organic average composition of the total capital of a certain society, *then the gradual and relative growth of the constant over the variable capital must necessarily lead to a gradual fall of the average rate of profit*, so long as the rate of surplus-value, or the intensity of exploitation of labour by capital, remains the same.

He goes on to say that one of the laws governing the capitalistic structure is that its growth implies a decline in the amount of variable capital as compared with constant capital and, thereby, a fall in the amount of variable capital relatively to the total amount of capital set in motion. He points out, moreover, that this relative decline in the amount of variable capital is nothing more than an expression of the progressive growth of the productive powers of society, which is shown by the fact that the same quantity of labor can, in the same time and through increasing application of machinery and fixed capital generally, work up an ever increasing quantity of raw and auxiliary materials, so that less labor is required to produce the same or a larger amount of goods.

Farther on, he adds that there can be not only varying rates of profit at different stages of development of a country but also varying rates of profit in different countries. The rate of profit, he says, is greater in the less developed countries.

Foreign trade tends to raise the rate of profit not only because it brings down the prices of foodstuffs but also because it contributes to the cheapening of constant capital and because capital invested in foreign and colonial trade yields a larger profit.

The extra profit resulting from the competition between capitals tends, eventually, to become a part of the general home rate of profit. This is what Marx called the superprofit, which he considered similar to the profit "of a manufacturer who exploits a new invention before it has become general."

I do not attempt to analyze the essence of Marx's theory (it would be out of place in this lecture), but I should like to emphasize that this brief outline of what is probably a contribution of Marx to economic theory—his discussion of the falling rate of profit—bears some resemblance to the way in which I have attempted to apply the principle of non-proportional growth between the factors of production, which is referred to as the principle of diminishing returns when applied at a given moment.

Some contemporary writers have arrived at a different mode of expressing certain general tendencies which closely resemble the one I have been dealing with hitherto. For instance, Mr. Keynes, in a chapter of his well-known *General Theory of Employment, Interest, and Money*, explains his concept of the "marginal efficiency of capital," which he defines as follows: "The relation between the prospective yield of a capital-asset and its supply price or replacement cost, *i.e* the relation between the prospective yield of one more unit of that type of capital and the cost of producing that unit, furnishes us with the marginal efficiency of capital of that type."

Thus defining the marginal efficiency of capital, Keynes explains how the yield of capital diminishes: "If there is an increased investment in any given type of capital during any period of time, the marginal efficiency of that type of capital will diminish as the investment in it is increased."

Finally, taking into account the fact that there could be no very great permanent divergence between the yield of invested capital and the current rate of interest, he sets down the relation between them as follows:

It is obvious that the actual rate of current investment will be pushed to the point where there is no longer any class of capital asset of which the marginal efficiency exceeds the current rate of interest. In other words, the rate of investment will be pushed to the point on the investment demand-schedule where the marginal efficiency of capital in general is equal to the market rate of interest.

Keynes considers, moreover, that his concept of the "marginal efficiency of capital" is the same as Marshall's "marginal utility of capital" and Professor Fisher's "rate of return over cost."[7]

Quite apart from Keynes's contributions to modern economic theory and his use of them to explain the trade cycle, it is clear, in his words, that the marginal efficiency of capital "will diminish as investment .... is increased"—a point which closely resembles Marx's argument that the rate of profits falls as the volume of constant capital increases. This resemblance has already been pointed out. Let me quote, for example, John Darnell, in an article entitled "The Economic Consequences of Mr. Keynes,"[8] where he says: "There is a teasing resemblance between Mr. Keynes' cyclical changes in the marginal efficiency of capital and the secular tendency for it to fall, with the Marxian fluctuations in the rate of profit and its tendency to fall."

However, for my own part, I merely wish to

[7] He quotes the main relevant passages in Marshall's *Principles* and then says: ".... Professor Fisher uses his 'rate of return over cost' in the same sense and for precisely the same purpose as I employ 'the marginal efficiency of capital.' "

[8] *Science and Society* I (1937), 205.

emphasize what I said before, namely, that in all probability the phenomena referred to by Keynes, Marx, and others are tantamount to that lack of proportionality in the growth of a nation's factors of production which I have already mentioned. To be more explicit: When a country has plentiful natural resources but little population and little capital, the latter will flow to that country to exploit its natural resources; and we find that in practice the three factors are growing more or less in proportion. It may even be that new land is discovered, new natural resources tapped. But eventually the rate of growth of population slows down, and there are no new resources to be discovered, whereas capital may continue to accumulate as before. Then, with natural resources more or less known, population more or less stationary, and capital still increasing, the returns to capital will be progressively lower—unless the other two factors can be increased once more. That is to say, once a certain stage is reached, a nation's capital grows much more rapidly than its other productive factors; hence the rate of profits or marginal efficiency of capital decreases as the lack of proportionality between capital and other factors increases—as classical economists anticipated.

Although later on I might dwell upon this subject at greater length and at my leisure, I mention this explanation in the hope that others, better equipped for the task than myself, may subject it to strict theoretical analysis and statistical proof. It seems safe to state, nevertheless, that the fall in the rate of profits at a given period in a nation's economic life leads capital to seek investment elsewhere—wherever the yield may be higher.

II

An important factor in Great Britain's early capitalistic development was the investment in that country of Continental capital. Amsterdam was the main financial center providing this capital up to the time when Great Britain became a creditor nation instead of a debtor one. Gradually, through her own accumulation of capital out of her trade and industry, she developed a capital market of her own, as Amsterdam and the Italian cities had done before her.

As long as the profits of her trade and industry could be reinvested within the country in new enterprises, Great Britain found herself more or less in a state of equilibrium. When her rate of capital accumulation exceeded the opportunities of profitable domestic reinvestment, this apparent equilibrium was disturbed, and she had to face the problem of employing her surplus capital beyond her borders. Her natural outlets were her colonies and dominions, already important trade centers in British economic life; but her capital, nevertheless, flowed to every continent. By the second half of the nineteenth century Great Britain had become the leading financial center of the world.

To quote Professor Clapham, "as a rule England gives credit to all the world, and takes none." He himself quotes John Ball as follows: "English credit supplied the capital of almost the whole world."

British industry profited by the export of capital, for it meant, ultimately, an export of goods. Britain financed its exports and paid cash for its imports. "Practically speaking . . . . England gives long credits on her exports, while the imports are paid for in ready money." In her haste to invest capital abroad, Britain was even confronted at times with a scarcity of funds to pay for her imports. "It was principally in America and the Dominions that capital export brought men, accompanied men, and followed men."[9]

[9] J. H. Clapham, *An Economic History of Modern Britain*, Vol. III: *Free Trade and Steel, 1850–1866*, p. 235: "The export of capital, so far as is known, was at its peak in 1872. The estimate for that year is £83,500,000. Emigration was at its peak, for that decade, in 1872 and 1873, having begun to move up in the slack trade years 1867–9 when capital exports were low. The net emigration was very low in 1876–8; and in those years the estimated export of capital account shows a small adverse balance, as has been seen. Britain, the estimate suggests, had rather less than nothing for foreign investment when the necessary steps had been taken to adjust a trade balance upset by the disastrous harvests of the late 'seventies and by the blocking of export channels by war, the growth of foreign industries, tariffs and the depreciation of silver. In effect, she had to sell a trifle of her foreign investments to pay for her way. Something similar had

INTER-AMERICAN SOLIDARITY

In view of the skepticism of many Americans to-day, and certain of their arguments, which were refuted some time ago by Professor Cassel in this same institute,[10] one may ask if in the course of Britain's lending epoch there was not some clair-voyant mind which foresaw the consequences of investing such large amounts of capital in new areas of the world. Were there no people who con-sidered it dangerous to invest capital in America for fear that the latter's rapid economic growth might make her a rival of Britain and dispute with her the first place in world trade? If there were, how far did they succeed in checking the flow of in-vestment, and thereby in hindering the develop-ment of the United States?

Turning again to Professor Clapham, we find that "the free-trade leaders did not suppose that Britain, with her new cheap food, her coal and iron and machines and capital, had entered on an eter-nity of industrial and commercial leadership. An

happened, though the facts are more obscure, in 1847–48, when famine called for abnormal imports and revolution shut European markets. It was not to happen again until after 1914. In 1879 and 1880 the heavy flow of men was resumed. It might be called a distress flow, though it was not of the old tragic sort. They were building 10,000 miles of railway a year in the United States and wanted men. Mean-while the capital position was being adjusted. From 1881, the country was at least able to keep the greater part of the earnings of its foreign investments abroad for fresh investments."

[10] "The Utility of Foreign Investments," in *Foreign Investments* (Lectures on the Harris Foundation, 1928 [Chicago: University of Chicago Press, 1928], pp. 34 ff).

age of leadership, yes, but how long?" For economic historians it is a commonplace that the industrial
development of the United States, especially the
so-called "railway age," was made possible by the
investment of British capital.

They knew about America, as their master Adam Smith
had known, when he faced the possibility of a transfer of the
capital of the Empire across the Atlantic *"in the course of little
more than a century." "Here,"* Cobden, not yet a politician,
had thought in 1835 as he looked from Laurel Hill over the
valley of the Monongahela where it flows north towards Pitts-
burgh, *"here will one day centre the civilisation, the wealth, the
power of the entire world."* "The people there," his newspaper
ally, *The Economist,* wrote in 1851, "have our knowledge, our
skill, and more than our activity . . . . they have an immense
continent at their command, and they continually receive
accessions of capital and population from England and from
every country in Europe. From the relative progress of the
two countries within the last sixty years, it may be inferred
that the superiority of the United States to England is ultimately as certain as the next eclipse" (*The Economist,* March
8, 1851).

However, judging by results, it would not appear
that this forecast of events ever prevented Great
Britain from playing an important role in American economic growth in the second half of the nineteenth century and the beginning of the twentieth.
Nor does it seem that America's amazing development has reacted unfavorably on trade between the
two nations; at the outset of the present conflict, or
even before, the volume of trade was far greater
than at the time of the *Economist's* forecast.

"Dutch, German, and above all, English capital flowed into the securities of American railroads—although the regularity of such investment was violently interrupted by panics or by the occasional disclosures of the folly of the American promoters."[11]

Thus we see that, when it was Great Britain's turn, nothing was able to prevent the investment of her savings abroad, whereby she contributed to the economic development of many parts of the world. Through her investments she probably sustained and increased her industrial life more than she would have done otherwise.

The economic history of the United States provides us with a more recent example of the significance of foreign investment. One could almost say that this has been the mainspring of her own development. What would have been the outcome if no foreign capital had been invested in America during the railway age? What would have been the extent of development and the standard of living?

Fortunately for this part of the world—endowed as it was with ample natural resources—economic development was made possible largely through the importation of foreign capital. As profits were accumulated in the eastern part of the United States, new areas began to be opened up in other parts of the country. Soule's phrase "Go west,

[11] Kirkland, *A History of American Economic Life*, p. 382.

young man, go west"—made popular by that now famous leading article in the *New York Tribune*— marked the beginning of an era which saw the active and widespread development of the American Union. Imports of manufactured goods fell gradually until the United States was able to manufacture at home practically all she needed.[12]

The United States was a debtor nation until the first World War, and thereafter became a creditor nation. She was able to fill the gaps in production left by European industrial nations during that war and was thus enabled to accumulate capital rapidly, thereby reaching that stage of economic maturity at which a country no longer needs to rely on the entry of foreign capital or at which its investments abroad counterbalance or exceed foreign investments within its borders. "Within the period from 1914 to 1918 was condensed a stage of growth that might otherwise have taken much longer, perhaps several decades."[13]

[12] Maurice Dobb describes this process of internal development in a nutshell: "While in America industrialization of the Atlantic seaboard came relatively early in the century, complete and developed industrial capitalism did not come to the West and South till relatively late. There is evidence, I think, to suggest that for most of the nineteenth century, U.S.A. capitalism was occupied with a form of 'internal colonialism,' in which the agricultural hinterland played the role of a colonial area to Big Capital entrenched in the East. At any rate, not until the turn of the century did U.S.A. cease to be on balance an *importer* of manufactured goods" (*Political Economy and Capitalism* [London, 1937], p. 247).

[13] E. M. Patterson, "The United States and the World Economy," in *Essays in Honour of Gustav Cassel* (London, 1933), p. 480.

This important change in the position of the United States was so rapid that it inevitably created great problems for the internal American economy, especially at the end of the first World War, when there was excess productive capacity and it was difficult to reduce abruptly the rate of output in the war industries. A gradual change-over followed, only to undergo a sudden jolt when the great depression supervened. I think one may safely assert that during this period the European loans floated in the United States following on the close of the first World War actually helped to retard the great depression.[14]

During a considerable period of her existence, the United States has solved the problems brought about by her state of economic maturity largely by the setting-up of new enterprises at home. This was possible owing to the growth of her population—both natural and that due to immigration—and through investment of capital in other countries. One may say, in a sense, that the role of the constant stream of immigrants was similar to that of labor employed abroad through the use of exported American capital; moreover, immigration implied an increase in consumption at home similar to that which occurred in those foreign countries in which the capital was invested—quite a different case from that of Great Britain.

[14] R. R. Kuczynski, "American Loans to Germany," in *Foreign Investments* (Lectures on the Harris Foundation, 1928), pp. 169 ff.

It would appear, therefore, that internal necessity compels the United States to seek outlets for its surplus capital. One important outlet has been provided in the past by immigration at home and investments abroad, and in our days practically only by the expansion of industry for national defense production; this is a temporary outlet for capital which would not have existed if there had been no rearmament program. Thus it appears that American capital, otherwise idle, instead of being faced with a period of stagnation and a very low rate of profits, may find itself earning, if not the excessive and much criticized profits of the last war, in any case a higher rate of profit than it would have obtained in other circumstances. But apart from this expansion, which is after all only a temporary outlet for the present glut of capital in the United States, and in so far as immigration diminishes and capital continues to be accumulated out of profits at home and net credits in the balance of international payments, a knotty problem will still confront the country, namely, that of maintaining prosperity and promoting recovery at home by means of investment abroad.

With little, if any, immigration, with population subject almost exclusively to natural increase, and with a more rapid accumulation of capital which seeks investment, it appears to me that this problem of foreign investment is of paramount importance to the United States. In fact, except for the relief afforded by the program of national defense, this country is bound to invest most of its available capital in other parts of the world, lest its home activities reach a point of stagnation and its foreign trade become paralyzed.

Given the inevitability of future American loans, what are the possibilities for American capital?

First, there is Europe. The lend-lease scheme is, indeed, a form of investment in Europe. Furthermore, when peace returns, Europe's devastated regions will offer opportunities for investment similar to those of the previous post-war period, when Germany was granted extensive loans. These loans had a double effect: they provided an outlet for idle capital which expected a safe yield from German bonds (loans were sometimes even oversubscribed in twenty-four hours) and, second, they rehabilitated a foreign market which had disappeared suddenly with the Armistice and the advent of peace.[15] Probably, these loans were the keystone to the solution of Germany's problems. Many people believe, too, that they were responsible for Europe's problems thereafter, for they made possible German rearmament and the new onslaught on European democracy. But it is equally likely that they were the mainstay of economic activity during the post-war era and that, had it not been for them, the great depression might have begun long before.

[15] *Ibid.*, pp. 169 ff.

Europe may become a new field for investment, just as America provided an outlet for European capital in the past. If the Axis powers win, and the United States has to come to terms with a victorious Germany, there would surely be a field for American investments in Europe, but would they be safe? For, if in the past Germany was able to rearm with the aid of foreign loans and to become practically the ruler of Europe, what would be outlook for American capital invested in a German-controlled Europe? Would such investment be desirable? If Germany loses, the outlook is somewhat different. America could then undertake the task of European reconstruction, and American capital would thus find a relatively easy outlet, though not so easy as in the past, and a relatively safe outlet, though not so safe as in the past, either. But, unfortunately, this prospect is not, so far as one can judge, near at hand.

Another possible investment field is Africa. But Africa has always been a sort of crossroads for the ruling powers of Europe. Even if a democratic victory made it possible for American capital to find investments in Africa in friendly co-operation with Great Britain, sooner or later new European conflicts would place American investors in Africa in jeopardy. Moreover, the outlook for the colonies in the post-war era, and the international problems which investment in Africa might imply for America, are as yet very uncertain quantities. The prospect, therefore, for private investment in Africa does not strike one as very hopeful.

What about the Far East? With a rising power filled with an insatiable lust for dominion, with its interests traditionally inimical to those of America and of the Western world in general, and with the present precarious position of other Western powers in the East, it does not seem that the prospects are likely to be any better than in any of the other continents I have mentioned. Of course, a great deal depends on whether the Axis powers win the war. If they do, and the United States has to deal with totalitarian victors, the outlook in the East is much the same as that in a German-dominated Europe. If the democracies win, the economic reconstruction of the East is in any case a difficult proposition; its problems would be so complex that American capitalists might well refrain from investing in that part of the world, perhaps leaving all responsibility as regards collaboration in the hands of the state.

There thus remains, apparently, no other area for investment except the American continent.

III

What is the position in Latin America?

The Latin-American countries are relatively new, and their capacity to absorb capital is therefore great. Total foreign long-term investments in Latin America, excluding intergovernmental debts, amounted at the outset of the first World War to about 7,000 million dollars, according to reliable estimates.[16] This total was made up as follows: Great Britain, 51 per cent; United States, 23 per cent; France, 15 per cent; and Germany, 11 per cent. Total investments increased after the war. In 1929–30 those of Great Britain and the United States alone (it is difficult to obtain reliable figures for France and Germany) were estimated at some 9,500 million dollars, America's share having risen to over 50 per cent. However, by 1936 the total had dropped to some 8,400 million dollars, relative shares remaining about the same.[17]

One must allow, of course, for the effects of the present war. Probably a large amount of European-owned Latin-American securities has been sold to American citizens, and in some cases to the citizens of the American republics themselves. It is evident, notwithstanding, that, however large these investments may appear, they are undoubtedly small in comparison with the potential absorption of capital by Latin America and the invest-

[16] See Appendix, Table 1.

[17] American direct and indirect investments in Latin America show an uninterrupted growth up to 1929. In 1897 they amounted to only 308 million dollars. By 1914 they had risen to 1,649 million dollars, reaching a maximum in 1929, when the sum total was 5,429 million dollars. They declined thereafter, amounting in 1939 to 4,012 million dollars (see Appendix, Table 2).

ment opportunities confronting American capital today.

What are the problems involved in investing in Latin America?

It is common knowledge that they refer mainly to the political influence acquired by foreign capitalists. The following are the factors which play important parts in the economic development of the Latin-American nations: (1) a potentially rich territory with great prospects for foreign investors; (2) an excessive labor supply, even if unskilled, combined with a low standard of living; (3) excessive political activity that attracts the best local elements, since it is the only type of activity in which they can excel; and (4) generally poor states, whose responsibilities are in proportion to the economic backwardness of the country.

When an important firm is established in a poor country, opening up a large source of wealth and providing employment for the inhabitants and revenue for the government, it is only natural and very human that those who represent the foreign investors feel that they enjoy a privileged economic position. It is not unnatural that the inhabitants of the country concerned realize the significance of such a position and that they little by little come to grant the foreign investor an economic influence which might, at a given moment, become a decisive political influence in the life of that country. It is thus not surprising that the majority of the conflicts involving foreign enterprises in Latin America spring from their disproportionate economic importance which, as I have said, almost inevitably becomes a political influence. This makes it easy for them to solve whatever problems may confront them, since the mere threat of closing down may mean the impoverishment of the working population and often a financial disaster for the government. When this state of affairs becomes a tradition, it is hardly surprising to find a country's history marked by political and social disturbances and even bloody revolutions, which are in many cases only an expression of the efforts of these countries to shake off the political influence of foreign capitalists. The Mexican revolution, for example, was not lacking in a strong feeling of nationalism and a certain defiance of foreign interests. And even such important events as the expropriation of the oil companies in Mexico was due, among other things, to a natural desire or instinct to eliminate the existence within the state of forces so powerful that they threatened the state's very existence. Can anyone wonder, then, that foreign capitalists have become involved in serious problems concerning the internal policy of the borrowing countries? If the population is passive and the government acquiescent, there is no problem for the foreign company; labor is unable to organize itself, taxes are too low in relation to companies' profits; and, as a result, salaries and taxes—the only contribution made by the foreign concern to the national income—are always low, and there cannot be any national capital formation. Thus, although the investor may not, in the first place, have had any intention to acquire such a measure of influence, nor the local people to grant it, the former does in fact exercise a hegemony which ultimately becomes irritating, intolerable, and hateful.

Fortunately, this state of affairs has undergone considerable change. The existence of not merely one isolated foreign enterprise but many lessens the privileged position of any one company, even though the collective hegemony of the investors may be overwhelming.

The Latin-American statesman has not always been the obedient tyrant who submits to the investors' demands for privilege. When government officials yield to bribery, investors can still maintain their hegemony, if they wish, but when officials do not yield to threats or accept bribes, frequent conflicts are likely to arise between the foreign investor and the government.

I am not suggesting that this is the present position of any or all the nations of Latin America, but I do say that this is a true picture of the difficult initial stages in a situation in which, psychologically, there are two dominant factors: on the one hand, the natural attitude of superiority assumed by the investor and, on the other, the natural resentment of a people who are moved to reaffirm their national existence and their sovereignty.

Mr. Frank Tannenbaum, who is a careful student of Latin America, says in his book *Whither Latin America?* (published in 1934): "It is an area where imperialism has expressed itself in all its forms, from direct annexation to subtle, indirect, economic penetration. On this stage have been fought large issues of national and international policy." Tannenbaum goes on to say that, broadly speaking, Latin America is destined to a kind of economic stagnation, because its industrial development depends upon "(1) its resources, (2) its population, (3) the speed and amount of its capital saving, and (4) its internal and external markets." In discussing each of these points, he arrives at a very pessimistic conclusion, quite contrary to my own.

Latin America suffers, in fact, from a lack of coal. "The entire area of Latin America probably has less than 1 per cent of the total coal resources of the world." This is in striking contrast to the United States, where roughly 40 per cent of the total world reserves of coal are found; moreover, besides being scarce, Latin-American resources are of poor quality and are scattered in small quantities and, with the exception of Chile, in inaccessible

[77]

places. By reason of this lack of coal, Latin America is bound not to develop any basic industry for the production of steel, which is the bone and sinew of modern industry.

Although Latin America has sufficient waterfalls to generate power and enough oil fields, neither is a suitable substitute for the reducing power of coal in the iron and steel industry. And, since it is not possible to create such an industry, Tannenbaum considers it inappropriate to produce hydroelectric power, because this can be used only in a manufacturing industry which relies on imported equipment and machinery and, above all, because the development of hydroelectric power "requires a very heavy initial investment."

With regard to oil he says that "the development of petroleum in the northern part of South America is not likely to contribute to any important industrial development in that area." Such a development is not possible either in Chile or in Brazil despite their possessing some of the largest iron-ore deposits in the world, or in Argentina, Uruguay, or Paraguay, except for the manufacture of consumption goods with imported fuel. This applies as well to Central America, the Caribbean, and Mexico. Cuban iron ore will continue to be sent to the United States, and Mexico's "small deposits of comparatively poor coal will mean in the future, as it has in the past, a small and insignificant industrial development when compared with the type of industrial establishment we have in the United States."

Moreover, industrialization, he says, is pointless, since the population does not need manufactured goods, owing to its economic backwardness. Where the population is of the European type, the factors of production necessary for industrial development do not exist—namely, coal, iron, and lumber. There is hardly any saving or accumulation of savings. Consequently, every possible type of investment has to be made with foreign capital which, in turn, capitalizes its profits and exports them. This export of profits occurs not only in mining, textile, and other similar industries but also in transport and in agricultural activities. "It is only in so far as the industrialists, manufacturers and agriculturalists become nationalized that they contribute to the development of a native middle class and, excepting in Chile, the Argentine and a few other minor instances, it is notorious that foreigners are few, they are temporary residents, and that they do not become citizens of the country." And except for Germans, Spaniards, and Portuguese who marry Latin Americans, "the capitalist as well as the capital remains foreign."

To complete this pessimistic picture of industrial development, Tannenbaum adds that what little investment of foreign capital already exists has been made on the basis of concessions, that when these change hands "the concessionaire continues to own the property and control it as long as the concession lasts," and that "this concession rarely becomes native." He concludes that "we must view this development of industrialism in the light of the type of financing and control that lies back of it, and we must reckon with the conflict that arises between foreign interests and local needs and aspirations that frequently develop in such a situation."

Moreover, when investments have not been made on the basis of concession, they have implied some form of monopoly, which is likely to assert itself in artificial increases of profits, achieved through price control. This control of prices further restricts the already limited market, whose buying power is entirely dependent on exports.

Finally, where there is no monopoly, there is excessive tariff protection. The part played by the latter is somewhat similar to that of monopoly, with the aggravating condition that it cannot be removed, because it provides the government with an important source of revenue.[18]

This state of undevelopment leads the governments, as may be expected, frequently to seek for eign loans to meet their constant budget deficits, and it causes them, moreover, frequently to default

[18] See Appendix, Table 3.

on their loans. "Up to 1926 there had been some 45 separate defaults involving practically every country and including approximately 100 different loans."[19] Consequently, Tannenbaum does not advise private investors to subscribe to government loans which, he says, have been employed in the "overdevelopment of certain aspects of the industrial mechanism—roads, railroads, harbours, etc.—which have, economically speaking, exceeded the immediate needs of the country and possibly their capacity for profitable operation." And, he adds: "If resources and population were developing at a sufficient rate, even a great disproportion in such essentials might be absorbed. But if the population is more or less stationary, and the economic resources are either meager or unavailable for other reasons, then the burden of an excessive development in one direction may prove a positive hindrance." All this in turn translates itself into unstable exchange rates, problems of taxation (especially tariff problems), a greater need of loans, and further taxation.

[19] Tannenbaum mentions the following examples. "Panama had a constant deficit between 1921 and 1927 amounting to 28 per cent of the total expenditure of the government; Salvador, between 1910 and 1926, showed a surplus for only 4 years; Costa Rica, for the same period showed a surplus for only 6 years; Argentina, between 1911 and 1923, shows a surplus for only one year; Ecuador, between 1919 and 1926, also had a surplus for only one year; Brazil, between 1899 and 1925, showed a surplus for only 9 years, and no adequate financial data for Brazil since 1921 are obtainable."

The position as regards foreign trade is not more promising, according to Tannenbaum. Although "the economic organization of most, perhaps of all, the countries under consideration is geared to the export and import trade . . . . Latin America is not merely exporting its surplus and importing luxuries" but exporting essential raw materials and importing many articles of consumption. Exports nearly always consist of one or very few commodities. There is a large degree of regional specialization. A single commodity often constitutes anything between 50 and 95 per cent of the total exports of a country. As regards imports, they consist, as I have stated, mainly of foreign manufactured goods, and they constitute the main articles of consumption in the country.

With one-commodity exports and practically indispensable imports, it is natural to find frequent problems relating to foreign trade, although over a period of thirty years "practically every country in Latin America, with the exception of Honduras, has shown an almost continuous favorable export balance."[20]

I have reproduced almost in its entirety this

[20] E.g.: "Ecuador and Mexico show a continuous favorable balance since 1901; Bolivia, Cuba, Peru and Salvador show each only one year of unfavorable trade balance between 1901–1930; Guatemala, Chile, Brazil, and Costa Rica show but two years of unfavorable trade balance in that time; Nicaragua and Salvador, three years; Uruguay, four years; and Colombia, between 1905–1930, only four years."

desolate picture because I believe myself to be in complete disagreement with Tannenbaum's conclusions. I therefore beg you to follow the following argument.

There has been relatively little investment in Latin America. What little there has been was made on the strength of concessions, monoplies, or excessive tariff protection. The important influence of foreign investors has led to the maintenance of wages which everyone finds very low by comparison with American standards. Foreign trade is not at all diversified. Latin-American countries import most of their consumption goods. The investor meets with political, labor, and economic problems, and even investors in government bonds find sooner or later that most of the Latin-American governments are in default.

Very well. But the more pessimistic the picture unveiled by Tannenbaum, the stronger becomes my own argument for leading Latin America out of this unpromising situation. If we were to deal with most of Tannenbaum's specific examples, we should find that in the majority of cases, if not in all, the facts which he seizes upon as reasons for making industrialization unfeasible and, consequently, investments inadvisable are precisely those which we should use in arguing the need for such investments.

For instance, suppose a railway is built in an

undeveloped country. If further investment does not stimulate wealth and production in the area served by the line, thereby giving rise to a demand for the transport of new products and to a larger capacity for consumption among the population, how can anyone expect that railway to become a profitable investment? Or, if it is profitable by reason of tariff protection, how can anyone expect it to promote the economic development of the country? And since it is railways that I am discussing, I should have needed to mention only the example of the majority of the railway companies in the United States: as in other parts of the world, they have passed through a crisis largely due to over-optimistic expectations as to the results of the investment, on the one hand, and, on the other, by these results falling notably short of normal, partly as a result of road transport competition.

If investment is based on monopoly, how can anyone expect a country to develop rapidly when the investor lays down as a condition of his investment an obstacle to development? In other words, how can a country be expected to accelerate its economic development if markets are artifically limited by means of excessive prices imposed by the monopolist?

And if industries grow up behind excessive tariffs, how is it possible for them to progress if they lack the stimulus of competition which would make them progress as in the case of a territory as large as that of the United States?

Tannenbaum may be right regarding the paucity of iron and coal deposits in Latin America, but he does not take into account that man's inventive genius may some day—and this dream may already have been realized—obtain the same results with petroleum, in one of its forms, as a reducer of iron ore. In this case his conclusion would be untenable.

What is there to prevent economic growth in Latin America from taking any possible form, apart from heavy industry? For instance, why should it not be possible to produce in Latin America all the chemicals obtainable from its vast resources, even though there be no large steel industry? Why should it not be possible to increase the purchasing power of the inhabitants by creating every kind of occupation that can provide a larger home consumption, so that industries may arise to produce for a market which, owing to insufficient purchasing power, not even American industries enjoy at present?[21] Why should it not be possible for the Latin-American population to become accustomed to modern comforts of life, such as run-

[21] With a little intelligence on the part of labor authorities, and some investment, the textile industries can provide both purchasing power and cloth for the inhabitants and, in some cases, like that of Mexico, can even achieve technical progress long overdue which might increase wages and cheapen the products.

ning water, good drainage, clothing made from every kind of textile material, if it is given sufficient purchasing power?

When Tannenbaum considers this most essential point, he reasons thus: There can be no industry because there is no coal and no iron. There is, of course, petroleum; and hydroelectric power can be generated. But we cannot have this because it requires an enormous investment. That is to say, there can be no large investments because there is no coal and no iron, and the only thing that we could have, namely, hydroelectric power, we cannot have because it requires a large investment. Tannenbaum is right, provided his assumption is true and so long as a more thorough examination of Latin America's resources does not reveal hidden and unsuspected deposits of iron ore, coal, or other materials that may in the future act as substitutes for iron and coal or become even more important than the latter.

I am willing to admit that, in so far as Tannenbaum's assumption is correct, it might not be possible to create heavy industries based on steel in every Latin-American country. But what is there to prevent the creation of industries which may utilize the power derived from waterfalls if the necessary investment is carried out? And what is there to prevent the integration of a great continental steel industry, making use of whatever necessary materials are to be found—iron ore wherever it is to be had, coal wherever it exists, etc.—and shipping the finished product from wherever it is economically possible? Mexico's west coast, for instance, has extensive iron-ore deposits which cannot contribute to integrate an industry in the interior, because distance renders their use unprofitable. But why should not these deposits form part of the iron and steel industry of the western states of America, at the same time as industry in the East may replace imports of iron by exports of iron ore or of coal to feed Mexico's present and future iron industry?

Perhaps I am not the only one to disagree with Tannenbaum, for only recently Brazil, with the aid of American capital, started to build a large iron foundry to exploit her iron deposits—"among the largest in the world"—which, according to Tannenbaum, could not provide "any important development of steel manufacture in that country because of the absence of coal."[22]

With regard to Latin-American defaults we could say a great deal. In the first place, I might mention the almost incredibly dubious origin of some of the debts and their extraordinary snowball formation. Second, the enormous cost at which some of these Latin-American loans have been floated—a question which has attracted notice

[22] Cf. J. F. Normano, *The Struggle for South America* (London, 1931), especially chap. v.

more than once in this country. Third, they represent only a small fraction of the total of the defaults of the world as a whole. And, lastly, the criterion applying to governmental debts in Latin America should be similar to that which Professor Cassel advised before the Harris Institute (1928) with regard to the problem of war debts:

> A general settlement of all war obligations on reasonable lines is . . . . a matter of very important interest for America. It must obviously be recognized as a paramount interest for the United States, as well as for civilized humanity at large, that political claims should not be forced beyond what is compatible with economic welfare, and that therefore with regard to war obligations, a solution should be arrived at, allowing the whole economic life of the world a fresh start and the best chances for a prosperous development.

If this is the criterion advised in dealing with war debts, which probably represent a very large proportion of total defaults of *real* investment, why should it not be applied similarly to other debts—of dubious origin—which are only a small fraction of the total?

It would appear to be obvious, then, that on the whole it might be best to invest in countries where it has been found possible to introduce some measure of social reform, which offers a basis for the treatment of labor problems. It is not inconceivable that the paradise dreamed of by investors, where the law gives no protection whatever to the worker and every advantage to the capitalist, may turn out to be, in the end, a fool's paradise, when labor seeks by violent means the solution which the law has denied to its problems.

It is possible, furthermore, that the Latin-American nations may achieve a national economic status if they establish a wisely conceived fiscal system to free their national treasuries from the cramping conditions imposed by any one isolated source of revenue, such as a one-line foreign trade, mining, etc., and if they step without delay toward the creation of central banks where necessary. This will provide a solid foundation for economic and monetary independence and for the creation of a possible national banking system, both of which are necessary conditions for the formation of national capital.

It also seems advisable that investors should endeavor to select national enterprises which employ as high a proportion as possible of national capital and that they should associate with such enterprises the new schemes they have conceived for investment and for the economic development of the nation. In any case, concessions in the form of free gifts are to be avoided, because they may be considered later on as assets by the concerns and even may be claimed as real investments.

If the investors aspire to show farsightedness, they might even advise and assist Latin-American countries to nationalize whatever important sources of economic wealth might be controlled by foreign interests, bringing to bear on these problems the forces of reason and the dictates of mutual convenience. Such propositions, based on easy terms and spread over a lengthy period, should attract the interested parties by reason of their liberality, thereby enabling the countries to have a wider range of their own national riches at their command for the welfare of the continent as a whole.

IV

But quite apart from the volume, nature, and ease of investment in Latin America it is possible to state one definite fact, namely, that Latin America buys from the United States more than it sells. This may be inferred from an examination of a partial balance of payments of the United States with Latin America.[23] If we look at payments on current account, we find that Latin America's purchases of goods and services from the United States exceeded its sales to this country by 123 million dollars in 1930,[24] by 22 million dollars in 1936, by 88 million dollars in 1937, and by 185 million dollars in 1938—all these being more or less normal years.

[23] United States Tariff Commission, *The Foreign Trade of Latin America, 1940.*

[24] The figure for 1929, although not recorded, is in all likelihood a net debit as well.

If Latin America has been able to meet these net debits on current account with the United States, the only explanation is that it has obtained on current or on capital account the necessary funds. If these sums have been received on current account, they have certainly been provided by the rest of the world and not by the United States. If any part of them has been received on capital account, the United States may have provided Latin America with part of that sum. At any rate, the fact that Europe as a whole has an import surplus[25] throws light on one of the ways in which Latin America has financed its net debit with the United States.

The second World War has dislocated the trade of the American continent. Imports from and exports to Europe have diminished, and it is not far-fetched to surmise that a time will come when there will be hardly any trade with Europe or, it may be, with the rest of the world. If this is to be the future of Latin-American trade, and assuming, of course, that it is in the interests of the United States to conserve the custom of the Latin-American nations, how is it possible for the latter to continue buying from the American Union more than they sell to it? Evidently, then, there is only one source which, under these circumstances, can help Latin America to recuperate and increase the purchasing

[25] Cf. League of Nations, *Europe's Trade* (Geneva, 1941), pp. 30–37.

power it has lost through the war. That source can be only the United States.

I hope no one will find himself in the position of Cobden, who, according to Egerton, had preached that England's chief concern with foreign nations was to trade with them, but it had turned out that the chief concern of foreign nations was *not* to trade with England.[26]

Impelled by forces inherent in America's economic development and by forces relating to present-day world-trade conditions, the United States is fated to buy from Latin America more than she has bought up to the present, unless she would risk cutting off her economic relations with the rest of the continent and restrict her activities to those of a nationalistic economy whose only outlet would be the wastefulness of war.

I believe, then, that I have pointed out how, as a result of the accumulation of capital in the American economy, the United States is inexorably destined to export large amounts of capital in order to preserve its internal equilibrium. In the past the United States has solved this problem by an almost endless increase in its industrial capacity—an increase made possible partly by immigration. Since this factor is possibly nonexistent or greatly dimin-

[26] H. Egerton, *A Short History of British Colonial Policy*, p. 5. Mentioned in William H. Langer, *The Diplomacy of Imperialism, 1890–1902* (New York, 1935), I, 76.

ished today, as long as savings continue to accumulate and they are not diverted to war purposes, the problem is more serious and urgent than ever.

This conclusion was arrived at by other lecturers at this university in 1928.[27] For instance, Henry K. Norton said:

> With half a billion dollars accumulating in the United States every year over and above our running expenses, our own capital needs, and the credit requirements of the developed countries of the world; with great areas such as China, Mexico, Central and South America earnestly desiring funds for development, the investment of these moneys in such backward countries is hardly to be avoided. It would be very delightful if loans to such countries could be made on the same credit basis as we make loans to England or . . . . Germany. But until we remold the world closer to our heart's desire this cannot be the case.[28]

Apart from the irony in the last remark, this is the same conclusion arrived at by a group of members of the Royal Institute of International Affairs in their book *The Problem of International Investment*, where, regarding the situation in 1937, they say:

> The United States, in other words, possesses an export surplus which would be consistent with a considerable volume of foreign lending, but at present her citizens, discouraged by the experience of the recent past, are not in a mood to lend abroad. . . . . Sooner or later, in one way or another, equilibrium must be restored, but there are really three different ways in which

[27] R. R. Kuczynski, *op. cit.*

[28] "Backward Countries as a Field for Investment," in *Foreign Investments* (Lectures on the Harris Foundation), p. 208.

this may be done: by a resumption of foreign lending by the United States; by a decline in her export trade; or by an increase in the volume of her imports.

The United States, then, must export capital, investing large amounts of it in private enterprises tending to develop the Latin-American economy. I think this is an unavoidable necessity if Latin America is to continue purchasing American goods and services at the rate at which she has purchased them up to the present. The United States must act thus if she does not wish to risk the stagnation of her economy and of world trade, which would lead to a depression similar to that of 1929. The United States must foresee at this moment the fall in world trade and must devote herself now to creating that purchasing power which war inevitably destroys. As I have stated, the necessary investment to create this purchasing-power cannot at present be made in Europe or in Africa or in the East. I conclude, then, that the United States is fated to create this purchasing-power by means of investments in Latin America.

You may even have to give your capital away, lest you become a modern Midas and witness the decline and fall of the United States in the midst of a golden age of plenty—with all your gold interred somewhere in the Union.

I say, then: get rid of your treasure—lend it, give it, throw it away—if you do not want to perish in the misery of plenty.

CONCLUSIONS

1. As a natural and inevitable result of economic laws, whose workings are beyond her control, the United States is bound to export capital.

2. Apart from the giving-away of capital implied in such wartime measures as the present "loans and leases," or even future "loans and gifts," capital cannot be exported at present to Europe, Africa, or the Far East.

3. Owing to reasons dictated by her own internal economy, and also to conditions prevailing today in international trade, the United States must inevitably export capital to Latin America.

4. Previous exports of capital in the form of private investments have met uncertain conditions brought about by labor difficulties, political conflicts with the governments concerned, and economic troubles arising out of the excessive political influence which foreign enterprises tend to acquire. Economic difficulties arise principally from the economic poverty of the countries—a reason which accounts for the frequent defaults on the part of Latin-American governments.

5. Latin America's consumption of United States goods and services has been paid for partly with the net credits which have accrued from her trade with the rest of the world.

6. In view of the present dislocation of international trade caused by war, either Latin America

must consume less United States goods and services or the United States must help Latin America to recuperate and raise its temporarily lost purchasing-power. This can best be achieved by purchases from and investments in Latin America. Purchases may be planned with a view to the future needs of Europe; the investment of private capital should aim at the economic development of Latin America.

7. Government purchases must not be made at prices lower than those offered by other possible buyers, because this apparent temporary advantage would militate against the building-up of Latin America's economic capacity, which is one of the ends of the United States economy. Moreover, such tactics would tend to produce political resentment, which must be avoided if the economic solidarity of the continent is to be achieved.

8. Private investors can avoid the problems of the past if they abstain from seeking privileges based on concessions, monopolies, or excessive tariff protection, as on former occasions, striving instead to bring about co-operation with the nationals of the countries concerned. In this way a greater harmony would be achieved, and it would be possible gradually to accumulate capital which could be employed for the purposes sought.

9. The past experience of British investment in the United States does not seem to confirm the

fears that Latin America may become an economic rival of the United States.

10. Even if they wish to do so, the Latin-American countries cannot prevent their own growth, for this obeys the fatalistic working of economic laws. But they can be prepared—by means of wise labor, fiscal, and banking laws—to prevent investments from causing detriment to their sovereignty.

In November, 1939, I made the following statement to an American journalist who was reporting on the first meeting of finance ministers, held in Guatemala: "I think the future of the United States is irrevocably linked to that of Latin America. It is up to them whether they want to be linked to a poor Latin America or a rich Latin America. With all the advantages that would accrue if they were linked to a rich Latin America, I do not see how they can abstain from giving such co-operation." As Henry Wallace has said, "America must choose."

I do not believe that there can be any doubt about the choice, and I do not think it is in any way inimical to any fundamental interest of the Americas; and the conclusions we have reached merely anticipate, I think, the shape of things to come. This is, perhaps, the sense of the following words from Deuteronomy: "And thou shalt lend unto many nations, and thou shalt not borrow. And the Lord shall make thee the head, and not the tail."

APPENDIX

TABLE 1*

FOREIGN LONG-TERM DIRECT AND PORTFOLIO
INVESTMENTS IN LATIN AMERICA†

(In millions of dollars)

COUNTRY	1913–14		1929–30		1936	
	Amount	%	Amount	%	Amount	%
Great Britain....	$3,677	51	$4,050	43	$3,494	41
United States....	1,649	23	5,429	57	4,930	59
France.........	1,080	15	....	.....	....	.....
Germany.......	836	11	....	.....	....	.....
Total.......	$7,242	100	$9,479‡	100	$8,424‡	100

* *Sources:* Royal Institute of International Affairs, *The Problem of International Investments;* Cleona Lewis, *America's Stake in International Investments;* U.S. Department of Commerce, *The Balance of International Payments of the United States;* and the *Economic Journal.* Conversion rates: £=$4.86; 1 mark=$0.22; 1 franc= $0.18.

† Excluding intergovernmental debts.

‡ Great Britain and United States only.

TABLE 2*

TOTAL AMERICAN LONG-TERM INVESTMENTS
DIRECT AND PORTFOLIO, 1897–1939
(In millions of dollars)

YEAR	WORLD	LATIN AMERICA	
		Amount	%
1897........	$ 685	$ 308	45.0
1908........	2,525	1,068	42.3
1914........	3,514	1,649	46.9
1919........	6,456	2,406	37.3
1924........	9,954	3,673	36.9
1929........	15,393	5,429	35.3
1930........	15,134	5,246	34.7
1931........	15,635	5,187	33.2
1932........	15,252	5,157	33.8
1933........	13,799	4,925	35.7
1934........	13,114	4,947	37.7
1935........	12,630	4,941	39.1
1936........	12,486	4,930	39.5
1937........	11,074	4,101	37.0
1938........	11,070	4,051	36.6
1939........	10,770	4,012	37.3

* *Sources:* 1897–1929: C. Lewis, *America's Stake in International Investments;* 1930–39: U.S. Department of Commerce, *The Balance of International Payments of the United States.*

TABLE 3*

ANALYSIS OF GOVERNMENT REVENUE IN THE AMERICAN NATIONS

COUNTRY	CURRENCY UNIT	REVENUE (IN MILLIONS)						PERCENTAGE OF TOTAL				
		Total	Import Duties	Export Duties	Income Tax	Industry and Commerce	Other Taxes	Import Duties	Export Duties	Income Tax	Industry and Commerce	Other Taxes
Argentina (1937)	Peso	983.4	292.7	.....	84.2	173.5	433.0	29.76	.....	8.56	17.64	44.04
Bolivia (1937)	Boliviano	209.1	32.6	18.0	12.6	6.9	130.0	16.29	9.00	6.30	3.45	64.96
Brazil (1937)	Milreis	3,218.5	999.1	.....	201.1	788.7	1,229.6	31.04	.....	6.25	24.50	38.21
Chile (1937)	Peso	1,436.7	720.9	0.6	147.7	136.0	431.5	50.18	0.04	10.28	9.47	30.03
Colombia (1938)	Peso	81.1	32.9	1.2	11.3	7.7	28.0	40.57	1.48	13.93	9.49	34.53
Costa Rica (1938)	Colon	32.8	14.7	4.1	.....	6.9	7.1	44.82	12.50	.....	21.04	21.64
Cuba (1937–38)	Peso	79.2	30.1	.....	3.6	5.9	29.6	38.01	.....	4.55	20.07	37.37
Dominican Republic (1938)	Dollar	11.7	4.9	0.1	.....	3.5	3.2	41.88	0.85	.....	29.91	27.36
Ecuador (1938)	Sucre	120.5	33.0	0.6	5.1	35.4	46.4	27.39	0.49	4.23	29.38	38.51
Guatemala (1936–37)	Quetzal	11.6	4.8	1.8	.....	2.1	2.9	41.38	15.52	.....	18.10	25.00
Haiti (1935–36)	Gourde	34.6	17.5	11.3	0.5	2.0	3.3	50.58	32.66	1.44	5.78	9.54
Honduras (1938–39)	Lempira	11.5	4.7	.....	.....	2.1	4.7	40.87	.....	.....	18.26	40.87
Mexico (1940)	Peso	515.4	90.5	49.1	55.9	117.5	202.2	17.57	9.53	10.85	22.81	39.24
Nicaragua (1937–38)	Cordoba	5.6	1.5	.....	.....	1.3	2.8	26.79	.....	.....	23.21	50.00
Panama (1937–38)	Balboa	18.8	6.8	0.3	.....	3.2	8.5	36.17	1.60	.....	17.02	45.21
Paraguay (1937–38)	Peso	920.2	480.1	49.3	.....	.....	390.8	52.17	5.36	.....	.....	42.47
Peru (1938)	Sol	165.5	36.8	18.7	13.0	21.6	75.6	22.24	11.30	7.85	12.93	45.68
El Salvador (1938–39)	Colon	19.1	8.6	.....	0.5	2.1	7.9	45.03	.....	2.62	10.99	41.36
Uruguay (1937)	Peso	82.1	24.2	.....	2.4	13.8	41.7	29.48	.....	2.92	16.81	50.79
Venezuela (1937–38)	Bolivar	236.4	80.1	.....	.....	37.0	119.3	33.88	.....	.....	15.65	50.47
Canada (1936–37)	Dollar (Can.)	452.1	90.0	.....	102.0	.....	260.1	19.91	.....	22.56	.....	57.53
United States (1937–38)	Dollar	7,293.6	463.0	.....	4,140.1	1,309.3	1,381.2	6.35	.....	56.76	17.95	18.94

* Source: League of Nations, *Public Finance Reports*; Mexico, Ministry of Finance.

RAW MATERIALS AND INTER-AMERICAN SOLIDARITY

By ARTHUR R. UPGREN
Professor of Economics, University of Minnesota

RAW MATERIALS AND INTER-AMERICAN SOLIDARITY

I

THIS paper is addressed to the raw-material problem of the Western Hemisphere in the light of the probable actual conditions of the immediate future and not in terms of anything that could be said even distantly to approach an ideal world. By "raw materials" is meant products, natural or processed, that are in that state in which they constitute the basic materials for modern industrial production. Thus jute manufactures and newsprint, which upon their import by the United States are classified as "finished manufactures," are taken, for the purposes of this paper, to be raw materials because they are products used in the industrial production of the United States and not products intended for consumption in the form in which imported. Similarly, nickel, tin, timber, and wood pulp, classified as semifinished manufactures, are also taken to be raw materials.

The probable conditions of the future that are of such great present concern are not those conditions that would be laid down in any blueprint for some ideal kind of American solidarity. In fact, it is probable that if it were not for these present world conditions inter-American solidarity would not be the subject of the Harris Institute meetings of 1941. Rather, the only conditions considered are the conditions of the very immediate or short-range future and the somewhat longer-range future that can to some extent be envisaged to emerge from the present uncertain state of world affairs and from particularly the defense program of the United States. Put in another way, the short-range future is that future that we shall experience in carrying through any program of inter-American defense and rearmament. For the people of the United States, therefore, this short-range future is nothing more than that future which coincides with the amount of time required to implement the present defense and rearmament program of the United States. In contrast, what is termed the long-range future is taken to be that period of time required in order to achieve the maximum amount of inter-American solidarity in a world in which aggressor nations do exist and in which totalitarian regimes are expected to continue in power and to remain a threat to the peace of the Western Hemisphere. However unsatisfactory for all of us these short-range and long-range periods of time may be, the limitation of the analysis to the periods as defined is most fruitful because they embrace that extent of time in which our problem of security *must* be solved. It is by this time almost wholly clear that the problem of inter-American solidarity is a problem of survival of a system not too much unlike the system that has prevailed for us for the last one hundred years. And it is also equally clear that, whatever the system of the future may be for this hemisphere, it must be developed in the face of a world in which armed force plays a dominant role. If there should be an opportunity for the Western Hemisphere to participate in some kind of world organization more closely along the democratic rather than the totalitarian pattern, the task of such an investigation must be left to those optimistic enough to believe that such an opportunity is soon to become an actuality.

There are three aspects of inter-American solidarity. One of these is economic solidarity, which in relation to raw materials is the subject of this paper. The other two are political solidarity and military solidarity. It is patent that in these days of total war abiding military solidarity is heavily based upon economic power to produce that kind of commodity that is called "heavy" industrial production, which spells power in modern warfare. Political solidarity, if it is meaningful in any other than a ritualistic sense and if it is to envisage something of a consistency that is heavier than that which is created by *ad hoc* conferences, in very large part must be dependent upon some kind of economic or military sanction. Of all possible sanctions an important one is an improved economic and productive system that, to be sure, can be secured by formal political arrangements.

The foremost required condition for inter-American solidarity, however, is not directly an economic condition at all but rather the condition of the powers of defense possessed by all the American nations and, because of its large share of the world's industrial capacity, the condition of the military defenses of the United States. At the present time economic and political solidarity are factors secondary to the great need for military power that can make *any* kind of solidarity possible. If first things are to be put first, then the realization of the defense and rearmament program of the United States is the *sine qua non* of any program of inter-American solidarity. Given satisfaction of this condition, there can then be a solidarity of the kind that is acceptable to the American nations, and that solidarity I shall define as "consultative and responsible solidarity." This point is important because it provides the needed orientation for the development of any satisfactory plan of inter-American solidarity. By this is meant the fact that the one test in the immediate future for any program whatever for the Western Hemisphere is the test of the contribution of such a program to the ability of the Western Hemisphere nations to carry through to completion the building of adequate means for its defense. We are not privileged to aim for the building of a program of solidarity that ignores conditions existing in the rest of the world. The conditions which now do exist account for this foremost limitation upon any program of solidarity. Therefore, whatever program is advanced for achieving inter-American *economic* solidarity must be a program that advances and does not, on balance, in any way retard the ability of the hemisphere to create the complete means needed for its unquestioned defense. Such an economic program within the narrower field of raw materials, to some people for example, is provided by a proposal for what may be called "synthetic production" by the United States of many materials now secured from overseas sources. It can quickly be pointed out that any large amount of synthetic production would further tax the capital and labor resources of the United States that are already so severely burdened by the defense effort, and therefore such a solution for the United States alone at once must be ruled out of consideration.

II

It is natural that a program aiming at the solution of pressing raw-material problems of the countries of the Western Hemisphere should start with a brief survey of the raw materials that are involved. These raw materials of a "raw-material program" consist of two classes. The first class includes raw materials of import; the second, raw materials of export. To countries that are primarily exporters of raw materials and, it may be added, importers of finished goods, the raw-material problem, of course, is the problem of "export raw materials." To countries preponderantly importers of raw materials and exporters of finished goods, the raw-material problem is largely a problem of "import raw materials." The division of the raw-material problem into these two major classifications also suggests the superficial solution of a program of complete inter-American self-sufficiency. To some people such a program appears easily capable of fulfilment by the simple assumption that resources now devoted to export raw-material production can be diverted to the production of import raw materials. This position can be supported by value figures that are in the very nature of the case closely in balance. Such a program again can be quickly dismissed for the reason that it would involve in its fulfilment a most serious drain upon total hemispheric resources that are needed in the present defense programs.

To follow this general twofold classification of the raw-material problem of the hemisphere which must be solved to achieve any program of economic solidarity and security, consideration may first be given to the import raw materials that vitally affect the economies of some of the countries of the hemisphere. Inasmuch as somewhat the greater share of the hemisphere's industrial production is found in the United States, the test of which raw materials are import needs may conveniently be made with the aid of import trade data for the United States.

Within the past generation there has been a very striking change in the imports of the United States. To show this change a comparison is made of the value of United States raw-material imports in 1937 with the average annual value of such imports in the five-year period 1901–5, or a generation ago. These data are provided in Table 1 and are arranged in rank order of the value of the imports in 1937. It may be noted that the selection of the year 1937 for recent data provides a reasonably "normal" year and one, also, in the case of trade figures for certain European countries to be presented below, reasonably free from the aberrations that resulted from Europe's most intense armament efforts of 1938 and 1939.

The striking changes in the imports of the United States in the past generation are the great increases in imports of rubber, sugar, coffee, paper, vegetable oils, silk, tin, wood pulp, and wool. Of these imports the annual value-increase in the case of rubber was over two hundred million dollars, and for each of the other commodities the annual import value-increase very roughly averaged about one hundred million dollars. The listed commodities included the most important individual raw-

TABLE 1

VALUE OF RAW-MATERIAL IMPORTS OF THE
UNITED STATES, 1937 AND 1901–5
(In millions of dollars)

Raw Material Imported	1937	Average, 1901–5
Rubber..................	$ 248	$ 35
Sugar...................	166	77
Coffee..................	151	69
Paper...................	137	4
Vegetable oils...........	112	7
Silk....................	107	45
Tin....................	104	22
Wood pulp.............	98	3
Wool..................	96	25
Total.............	$1,219	$287
Percentage of total imports	40	30
Percentage represented by list exclusive of sugar, coffee, silk, wool.......	23	7

material imports of the United States. For the present problem it is highly significant to observe that, of the nine items, only two—coffee and paper —are secured preponderantly from countries of the Western Hemisphere and but one—wood pulp—is so secured from Europe. United States imports of the remaining six commodities are secured primarily from regions located in southeastern Asia, including Australasia.

TABLE 2

VALUE OF EXPORT COMMODITIES IN THE
UNITED STATES, 1937 AND 1901–5
(In millions of dollars)

Commodity Exported	1937	Average, 1901–5
Machinery..............	$ 479	$ 78
Petroleum.............	376	82
Automobiles............	347	....
Iron and steel..........	300	33
Total..............	$1,502	$193
Percentage of total exports	45	13
Cotton................	$ 369	$335
Edible animal products...	43	182
Wheat................	64	131
Total.............	$ 476	$648
Percentage of total exports	14	45

In the same period of thirty-five years an even more striking change has taken place in the export position of the United States. This can be illustrated by the data for seven export commodities. These data are given in Table 2 and are for the same periods covered by the import data given in Table 1.

In the first five years of the present century United States total exports of only three commodities—cotton, meat, and wheat—averaged $648,-000,000 annually and constituted no less than 45 per cent of total exports. In contrast, these commodities in 1937 accounted for only 14 per cent of total exports. In 1937 the new and most important exports of the United States were machinery, petroleum, automobiles, and iron and steel. These four commodities alone now account for no less than 45 per cent of total United States exports in contrast to only 13 per cent at the turn of the century. In other words, in relative shares the new great exports have exactly succeeded the earlier great roles of Kings Cotton, Wheat, and Meat.

It is also interesting to observe that over the same period of time United States exports of foodstuffs as a group declined from $490,000,000 to $283,000,000, or by 42 per cent. United States imports of foodstuffs, in contrast, increased from $246,000,000 to $853,000,000—an increase of not less than 247 per cent. In fact, United States imports of foodstuffs rather closely approach in value the total import of crude and semifinished goods.

With rising productivity and incomes in general over the entire world, ability to purchase durable goods is increased more rapidly than the increase in incomes. In high-income countries such purchases are made out of savings; in other countries they can be made because there is created a margin over and above subsistence. Long-run adjustment of foreign trade of the United States will probably be more favorably facilitated by pursuing such export lines than by attempting to revive agricultural exports. The absorption of increased raw-material imports by the United States and its export of machinery each contributes greatly, of course, to rising world productivity.

This brief representation of the main long-term changes in trade trends of the United States shows that export has become very largely an export of finished products that are produced with the aid of huge amounts of capital and a minimum of labor and that the import has become largely an import of raw materials that require in their production huge amounts of labor and a minimum amount of capital. If a detailed study were made of the labor amounts involved, for example, in the trade between the United States and the area of southeastern Asia, it might show that the exports sold to that area involve the labor of no more than about 500,000 workers, while the imports might represent the labor of probably no less than about 15,000,000 workers. We shall test at a later point the adequacy of areas of the Western Hemisphere to meet the productive requirements of the United States that are secured from this other great raw-material-producing area of the world.

This position (exclusively for the United States) has been given in order to show that the ability of the United States to produce for domestic and export requirements lies importantly in such commodities as machinery, petroleum, automobiles, and iron and steel. It is not without significance that ability to produce these four commodities is the major test of ability to carry through to a successful conclusion either an adequate defense program or even total war. In contrast, the great need of imports by the United States is for supplies of rubber, paper, vegetable oils, tin, and many commodities, some of which are of high strategic importance though perhaps of low import value, including antimony, tungsten, chromium, graphite, mica, quinine, jute, and manilla. Thus a program of inter-American solidarity that is dependent upon the armament-producing ability of the United States must maintain, and must maintain economically now that United States resources are to be used to the full, adequate supplies of all these vital raw materials.

III

In juxtaposition to the central problem of maintaining imports for the United States there is the second and equally important problem of maintaining export outlets for the raw-material-producing countries of the hemisphere. As is so well known, there is only one important agricultural-deficit area in the world—western Europe—and there are only two outstanding world industrial areas consuming the world's raw-material production (other than foodstuffs and feedstuffs). The latter two areas are the highly industrialized areas of western Europe and of North America. The great need of the lesser industrialized Western Hemisphere areas for export markets is emphasized because of the fact that the import problems of these raw-material-producing areas involving the import of finished goods can largely be resolved by the export power of the United States. With such finished-goods imports there should be included an increasing ability to supply technical implements of war for which the United States is developing what should soon become adequate capacity. But before turning to the raw-material export requirements of the countries of the Western Hemisphere, it is desirable briefly to review the total trade situation of the hemisphere as a whole.

In 1937 the value of total exports of all countries of the Western Hemisphere amounted to $6,790,000,000. Of this amount of total hemispheric exports, $2,656,000,000 was consigned to countries within the hemisphere. Thus the intra-hemisphere market absorbed 39 per cent of the total exports originating in all countries of the hemisphere.[1] The significance of this percentage of hemispheric absorption of hemisphere exports is partially revealed by a comparison with the corresponding position of Europe. In the case of Europe, in contrast, no less than 64 per cent of total exports were consigned by the countries of Europe to other countries within Europe.[2] Thus an assumed policy of hemispheric isolation to achieve solidarity would result in a much more violent foreign-trade readjustment for the hemisphere than would be required in the case of isolation for Europe. Moreover, the range of important export products of the Western Hemisphere tends to be very limited compared with Europe; this is owing to the fact that the Western Hemisphere's export products consist in large part of a few important world staples such as meat and wheat, copper and cotton, petroleum and feedstuffs. In contrast, the exports of Europe are primarily widely diversified finished products.[3] In addition, there is a further

[1] Based upon data contained in *Foreign Commerce Yearbook, 1938*.

[2] League of Nations, *Europe's Trade* (Geneva, 1941), p. 7.

[3] It may be said that a description of the effects of a policy of complete isolation for any unified area may compare the intra-area exports that would be lost either with (1) total exports or with (2) total production. It is perfectly true that the extent or depth of an economic adjustment is to be measured by the proportion of (1) the sacrificed exports to (2) total production. Nevertheless, because the total exports of many countries of the Western Hemisphere constitute such a very high proportion of their total production, the comparison of the

telling argument to show that a policy of isolation would probably result in far more hardship for the Western Hemisphere than would be true for Europe. This point is that the production of the great staples of the Western Hemisphere is carried on in monoculture areas. In contrast, Europe's export of finished products is an export of products of "multiculture" areas. This is so because finished products so important for Europe are so commonly the products of urban industrial communities where workers have many alternative opportunities for productive effort and where even capital is generally less specialized and has a higher rate of depreciation than is true in the case of the largely "land capital" of raw-material countries. Finally, the finished industrial products of the industrialized countries of Europe are very largely goods of high-demand elasticity, whereas many of the staples of Western Hemisphere countries are goods of low-demand elasticity. Thus again a policy of isolation would work much greater hardship upon the countries of the Western Hemisphere than would be true in the case of Europe. The Western Hemisphere in the discernible future seems quite unable to consume all of its tobacco, cotton, wheat,

---

total proportion of export volume that would be lost, assuming complete isolation, is reasonably valid and it is, of course, a much easier fact to establish. In the case of Europe, however, the share of (1) the exports to (2) total production is generally smaller than is the case for most of the countries of the Western Hemisphere.

petroleum, and probably much of its meat and feedstuffs. In contrast, it would probably be much easier for the industrial nations of Europe to find or develop more nearly adequate markets within Europe for their finished products such as iron and steel, films, clocks and watches, earthenware and china, glass and glassware, paper and wood manufactures, and butter and eggs.[4]

Turning to the total import position of the Western Hemisphere, it is found that the total amount of the imports of all countries of the hemisphere is $5,601,000,000, of which $2,385,000,000 is secured from countries within the hemisphere. Thus, tested by imports, 43 per cent of the hemisphere's imports (1937) are secured within the hemisphere. Accordingly, a policy of complete isolation would cause an immediate loss to the hemisphere of 57 per cent of its imports. In the case of Europe, since 54 per cent of import requirements are secured from countries of Europe, complete isolation would cost only 46 per cent of Europe's total imports.

The scope of this paper does not permit an examination of critical and strategic needs of Europe that must be satisfied from non-European sources. But, given access by Europe to the Mediterranean area and the Near East and given opportunity to develop Russian resources, the list of needs that the

[4] See Carl Major Wright, *Economic Adaptation to a Changing World Market* (Copenhagen, Denmark: Munksgaard, 1939).

European area as enlarged could not satisfy is surprisingly short indeed. It includes two value-important commodities—fats and oils and feedstuffs—in the event that supplies from Russia were not adequate. A satisfactory development of the superabundant oil reserves of countries of the Near East is assumed, as is a reasonably satisfactory solution of the textile-fiber problem in the event that additional production from Russian areas was not adequate. The list of commodities which this enlarged European area would lack—commodities that are of strategic if not value importance—includes antimony, tungsten, and tin, products also not available in adequate amounts within the Western Hemisphere area. Finally, additional deficiencies in the case of Europe would include nickel, copper (if substitute production is not adequate), and probably vanadium and lead. These commodities are available in adequate amounts within the Western Hemisphere area, but their deficiency up to the present time in the case of blockaded Europe has not appeared to cause any unusual difficulties.

IV

In order to approach our central problem, a list of what may be called "net exports" and "net imports" of raw materials, primarily, for the Western Hemisphere may be determined under the assumption that the countries of the hemisphere maximize their purchases from each other. By this assumption is meant either (1) that any country of the hemisphere which has an import of any commodity of which some other country in the hemisphere has an export would purchase its total net import volume from such other countries of the hemisphere if such export exceeded the import volume or (2) that such a country would purchase the total export volume of the exporting countries if such export volume is smaller than the import need of the first country. On the basis of this assumption, the realization of all potentially complementary trade, the countries of the Western Hemisphere could increase the share of their imports secured from within the hemisphere to 65 per cent, in comparison with the present actual intra-area import share of 43 per cent. In the case of exports such maximization of intra-area trade could increase the proportion of the hemisphere's total exports which are absorbed within the hemisphere to 54 per cent from 39 per cent, the present share.

It is interesting to compare the proportion of total hemispheric exports that could be absorbed within the hemisphere with a similar figure for the area of Europe, including all Mediterranean countries and the Near East, but exclusive of Russia. In the case of the Western Hemisphere ability to absorb 54 per cent of total exports has been shown.

The corresponding figure for the total exports of the area of Europe, as defined, is 79 per cent. The figures for imports are 65 per cent for the Western Hemisphere and 69 per cent for Europe. Thus a very marked superiority is shown in the case of Europe. Because of the fact that the total trade of the countries of Europe is about one-half again as large as the trade of the Western Hemisphere, the proportion of the trade that would be lost by "area isolation" is probably a greater figure in the case of Europe in relation to either the total national income of the countries of Europe or the total annual value of all production.

Net imports of the hemisphere as they have now been defined represent what is in effect the net draft of the Western Hemisphere upon the rest of the world after first utilizing fully its own hemispheric supplies. Such leading net imports are given in Table 3.

The net raw-material imports listed above, amounting to $979,000,000, may be taken as representative of the normal annual import requirements of the Western Hemisphere for the commodities given. In addition, it is interesting to observe that there is a very large net import of $224,-000,000 of finished cotton and wool textiles and clothing and an import of ceramics and glassware (given for illustrative purposes) amounting to $34,-000,000. The list contains a redundant final amount of all other net imports—$633,000,000—which is a catch-all classification for all unlisted exports and

TABLE 3

VALUE OF NET RAW-MATERIAL
IMPORTS OF THE WESTERN
HEMISPHERE, 1937

Net Raw-Material Imports of the Western Hemisphere	Value in 1937 (In Millions of Dollars)
Rubber..................	$270
Silk and rayon..........:	142
Vegetable oils and fats....	134
Jute and other vegetable fi- bers.................	103
Tin....................	78
Sugar..................	57
Furs...................	57
Pulp and pulp wood......	40
Tea....................	32
Cacao beans.............	22
Coal and coke..........	22
Wool..................	13
Iron ore...............	9
Total.................	$979

It is interesting to observe that two important non-raw-material imports include:

Cotton and wool textiles and clothing..........	$224
Earthenware and china, glass and glassware.....	34
All other net imports.....	633
Grand total..........	$1,870

imports, largely a net import balance of a very widely diversified list of manufactures imported chiefly from Europe and a diversified list of agricultural and raw-material products that individually are not so important in value terms as the detailed commodities given in the first section of the table.

A review of the thirteen individual raw-material and agricultural products given in Table 3 will serve to reveal the import raw-material problem of the Western Hemisphere. There are a number of commodities of which satisfactory hemisphere supplies could undoubtedly be developed. These include the small net imports of iron ore, wool, and coal and coke and may be eliminated from serious consideration. The items of intermediate importance include the last five items of cacao beans, tea, pulp and pulp wood, furs, and sugar. In connection with these it may be pointed out that about one-half of the hemisphere's requirements of cacao beans are produced within the hemisphere. Therefore, with this large existent production, it would seem quite possible to produce all the hemisphere's requirements. In the case of tea there is apparently no appreciable production within the Western Hemisphere, although there is a substitute in Brazilian tea (yerba maté) highly preferred in many areas and by many people of the hemisphere. The import commodity of pulp and pulp wood does not represent serious difficulty inasmuch as probably adequate although somewhat higher-cost supplies could be made available with enlarged Canadian production. The net import of sugar by the Western Hemisphere is derived by subtracting from the much larger value of sugar imported by the United States from the Philippine Islands the fairly substantial value of sugar export by the hemisphere to European countries. In fact, were the United States to make arrangements to absorb the export production of the southern part of the hemisphere as well as the rather large export production of the foreign possessions in the Caribbean, the hemisphere, of course, could very easily become wholly self-sufficient in sugar.

As a result of this review of import commodities of minor and intermediate importance, there remain five very large net imports of the hemisphere —rubber, silk and rayon, vegetable oils and fats, jute and other vegetable fibers, and tin. Each of these important imports is preponderantly absorbed by the United States and is almost entirely secured from southeastern Asia, including, in the case of silk and rayon, Japan within that area. In the case of tin the provision of adequate smelting facilities in the United States together with either an increase of production in Bolivia or an economizing of consumption of tin by the United States could probably solve the tin problem. In addition, the very large import of silk could probably, though not without inconvenience, be dispensed with in favor of enlarged hemispheric production of artificial substitutes. The present imports of rayon could undoubtedly be domestically replaced by a reasonably moderate expansion of the hemisphere's rayon industry.

But the nub of the problem for the Western Hemisphere is uncovered when the hemisphere faces the net import problem represented by jute, vegetable oils and fats, and rubber. The process of producing jute fiber, for example, is voracious in its demand for labor. It is probably quite accurate to say that if the low cost and large supplies of labor in British India were not available for the production of jute the Western Hemisphere would not have jute. If it were at all possible to establish jute production within the Western Hemisphere, it is certainly very questionable whether labor resources would be adequate and certainly either labor incomes for such effort would be very much lower or the cost of jute would be very much higher. Proposals to substitute cotton for jute have been made many times in the United States. It has been demonstrated that such a proposal would cost American agriculture more than it would gain. In addition, any program of greater Western Hemisphere self-sufficiency would require a very tremendous expansion of its cotton and wool textile and clothing industry. In view of its present defense effort, the Western Hemisphere does not have productive resources sufficient both for such a great enlargement of its textile industry and for the provision of jute substitutes. Finally, in the interest of hemisphere solidarity, there has frequently been the proposal that, because rubber production is from a tree indigenous to the Western Hemisphere, it might be productively restored to its original location. One such proposal envisages the establishment in the favorable potential rubber-growing areas of Central and South America of a production based upon small unit farms equivalent in extent to two or three acres. But if a comparison is made of the land areas of the Western Hemisphere appropriate for rubber production with the areas possessing an adequate population for undertaking the proposed small farm unit production of rubber, it will be found that the two areas are very distinctly much more mutually exclusive than coextensive. Practically the same situation exists in the case of vegetable oils and fats. The fact must be frankly realized that the Western Hemisphere trade of its labor-economizing products for the labor-using products of the far eastern areas has been a most economical trade. Rubber and some of the vegetable oils and fats could be produced in the Western Hemisphere, but the higher cost of such supplies (let alone the undoubted lack of labor resources sufficient for their production within the Western Hemisphere in sufficient amounts) deters the making of such a proposal. In the case of jute, vegetable fats and oils, and rubber this production is now carried on in areas of immense population resources trained to labor in full tropical areas. Similar population resources in adequate amounts for the needed production do not exist anywhere in the Western Hemisphere. The only solution that can be suggested as at all feasible is to develop such production in appropriate areas of the hemisphere with the aid of labor-saving machinery produced in the industrial areas of the hemisphere. In the event of an adverse outcome of the war, resort to such a solution might be necessary. But it must be perfectly clear that during the present rearmament effort the industrialized areas of the Western Hemisphere cannot spare capital resources for such an effort.

The very much greater burden of the export problem is at once revealed when attention is directed to the net exports of the Western Hemisphere. The leading net exports of raw materials and agricultural products are given in Table 4.

A survey of the foregoing list of net exports of the Western Hemisphere reveals the immensity of the export problem of the hemisphere. Taken as a whole, the hemisphere, after a maximum absorption of its own raw-material production, has no less than $2,300,000,000 of export surpluses of the fourteen listed commodities, and there is in addition the very great export by the industrialized areas of machinery and vehicles in the amount of $518,000,-000. Thus for reasonable prosperity the export sur-

TABLE 4

VALUE OF NET RAW-MATERIAL
EXPORTS OF THE WESTERN
HEMISPHERE, 1937

Net Raw-Material Exports of the Western Hemisphere	Value in 1937 (In Millions of Dollars)
Grains, including flour....	$458
Cotton................	427
Petroleum..............	426
Copper................	223
Nonferrous metals other than copper and tin....	121
Cattle, swine, meats......	173
Tobacco...............	136
Timber and lumber......	86
Coffee.................	72
Iron and steel..........	71
Oil seeds..............	48
Vegetables, fruits, and nuts	33
Hides and leather........	24
Fertilizers.............	13
Total................	$2,311

In addition to the foregoing raw-material commodities, important net export surpluses of the hemisphere include:

Machinery and vehicles...	$ 518
Rubber manufactures....	36
Miscellaneous metal products................	32
Grand total..........	$2,897

pluses of the hemisphere must total almost $3,000,-000,000. This is in contrast to import surpluses as already shown, amounting to only $2,000,000,000 and consisting in rather substantial part of a very wide range of finished products, the production of which the hemisphere itself could probably reasonably well manage at home. It has been shown that the hemisphere has a most serious import problem in the case of rubber, vegetable oils and fats, jute, and tin. But the total value of these imports is only about $600,000,000. In contrast, the hemisphere normally wishes to export more than $400,000,000 in grains, a like value of cotton, and a like value of petroleum. The hemisphere also normally exports no less than $350,000,000 of nonferrous metals, $200,000,000 of animal products (edible and inedible), a very substantial amount of tobacco, and large amounts of timber, coffee, oil seeds, and vegetables, fruits, and nuts, and finally machinery and vehicles in an amount of over $500,000,000.

In the light of this huge export problem and in the light of the very substantial import problem of the Western Hemisphere, what solutions, in the interest of inter-American solidarity, can be proposed?

V

The raw-materials problem from the point of view of inter-American solidarity has now been presented as the problem of a few imports of substantial value and volume and an even greater value and volume of raw-material exports. Consideration may now be given to the solution of this twofold problem.

The first solution that may be proposed for achieving greater Western Hemisphere solidarity is a solution that may be described as "trade integration." The application of this solution might involve the creation by inter-American action of either a complete customs union or a substantial degree of reciprocal tariff preference for the products of the hemisphere. This solution would not be satisfactory, however, because the method is quite inapplicable with respect to a great many raw materials that constitute almost the only exports of many countries of the hemisphere. It is inapplicable because a very large proportion of such commodity trade is free rather than dutiable. Without tariffs neither a complete customs union nor a preferential system has any significance. Coffee, bananas, tin, certain types of hides and skins, sausage casings, sisal, cacao beans, nitrates, and newsprint, for example, are admitted by the heaviest-consuming area—the United States—quite free of duty. Thus tariff action per se cannot stimulate any greater intra-area trade in these "free" commodities. In addition, in so far as either tariff elimination or tariff preference is feasible, the hemisphere, organized as a preferential area, would find that, taken as a unit, it possessed great export surpluses the markets for which are outside in world markets. This was the lesson learned by the raw-material-producing areas of the British Empire under its preferential system. Because such areas had an export production that had to be sold in markets outside the empire, the price for such goods within the empire-consuming areas could be no higher than the price that obtained in the world market. In view of the huge export surpluses of the Western Hemisphere, a preferential system for this area would merely accentuate in an accumulated hemisphere surplus the present country surpluses.

A second proposed solution, one to some extent already considered, is the readjustment of exports and imports in order to increase the degree of complementarism in hemisphere trade. This, it might be said, could be accomplished in part by a reduction of tariffs by the United States, for example, on those goods which it produces but of which there is a large and more efficient production in other countries of the hemisphere. Such tariff action, however, would not assure a large market in the United States for the raw-material products of other hemisphere countries. This is owing to the fact that the effect of the tariff reduction might well prove to be only an alteration in the price at which the internal production of the United States would be sold in the domestic markets rather than the effect being an increase in the import value of such raw-material products secured at the expense of United States production. In other words, the reduction in the tariff on a given commodity produced in the United States does not assure United States markets to other countries. If there are no alternative lines open for United States producers, a price adjustment by domestic producers to the new conditions created by the tariff reduction could be effective in their retention of the domestic market.

But this second proposed solution of a readjustment of exports and imports could be made effective if it were managed by the allocation of purchase quotas to firms in some countries of the hemisphere for the entry of their products into other countries of the hemisphere with appropriate readjustment or control of similar domestic production. Certainly readjustment of this kind to improve the intrahemisphere markets for some countries whose world markets have been largely lost as a result of the war is desirable. The test for such action is the judgment that failure to take it leads to consequences that are more serious than those that would result from such action. Here can be seen the need for more constant consultative procedures and institutional arrangements than are provided by *ad hoc* conferences.

If this second solution of readjusting export and import lines is envisaged as a solution intended to provide complete economic solidarity for the American countries, then it becomes a program of self-sufficiency and economic isolation. Some of the implications of such a program have already been considered. The principal objection that has been advanced in the light of the conditions now faced by the hemisphere is that eliminating hemispheric export surplus lines and instituting production of commodities now imported from the outside world is a herculean task. Human resources that would have to be transferred do not possess complete personal mobility. Moreover, the development of a substitute hemispheric production for present raw-material imports from the outside world, particularly from southeastern Asia, would have to be located very largely in the tropical areas of the hemisphere, while the human resources of this hemisphere, unfortunately, are very largely found in the temperate areas. Thus, even if there were fluidity of adaptable labor, there would still be required a new complement of houses, roads, railways, communication and shipping facilities, etc., in the tropical areas and a sacrifice of similar facilities now existing in the temperate-climate areas. Finally, there is the most telling argument that, since the hemisphere is now engaged in a gigantic defense effort involving huge drafts upon its present capital and labor resources, the most serious cost of readjusting present production would be the achievement of that very rearmament effort itself.

A third solution for the problem of raw materials and inter-American solidarity can be proposed. It is a solution having two main complementary policies. The first aspect of this solution is the maintenance of the fullest possible output by the industrialized areas of the hemisphere. With the maintenance of such full output the utilization of the raw materials of the hemisphere is kept at a maximum. If the industrialized areas could consistently maintain a reasonably full output, their absorption of hemispheric raw-material production could be greatly increased from the levels of the past decades. Such increases could aid present raw-material production lines and provide an opportunity to develop new complementary lines to satisfy the growing industrial demand. Copper provides an excellent illustration. Only a few years ago the United States imposed tariff restrictions on the import of copper in order to protect its own copper industry then operating at very substantially less than capacity. As a result of the greatly increased level of production in the United States—much of it armaments, to be sure—consumption of copper which in some of the low years of the 1930's was less than 500,000 tons will apparently be increased to a consumption as high as 1,500,000 tons. As a result of its ability to consume much more copper and as a result of full employment of domestic copper-producing resources, the United States is now preparing to import very substantial amounts of copper. In fact, there are strikingly close correlations between the levels of industrial production within the United States and its volume of raw-material imports. Most of such imports enter free of duty so that tariff reduction is quite inapplicable. Consequently, with increasing production within the United States there should be increasingly improved markets for many other raw materials of the hemisphere. In fact, the very ability of the United States to play a role in world affairs as well as in the Western Hemisphere is probably more dependent upon maintaining a vigorously producing economy than upon any other single line of action.

The second aspect of this third solution is the maintenance of as free as possible a trade with other specialized raw-material areas of the world that are not yet victims of the rampant forces of aggression. Another such area is the specialized raw-material-producing area of southeastern Asia. There is an excellent illustration of the present importance of the specialized raw-material production of the Far East to the Western Hemisphere, particularly, to be sure, the United States. This illustration is provided by rubber. The United States annually imports about 500,000 and never more than 600,000 tons of rubber. Because of the present enlarged consumption of the United States, requirements for rubber in the first six months of 1941 were at the annual rate of 817,000 tons. Certainly a hemispheric program of self-sufficiency in rubber would be most difficult at a time when hemispheric consumption is advancing by leaps and bounds. Consequently, it is most important for the hemisphere to be able to tap the production of specialized world areas rather than to weaken itself by attempting to develop alternative sources of supply. Only by providing a close integration with both important raw-material-producing areas that have been reviewed so briefly can the United States and the Western Hemisphere as well (because of the centralization of industrial power in the United States) face the future with confidence.

Finally, the greatest single food- and raw-material-importing area of the world—Britain—still free from conquest, should be preserved in order to minimize the Western Hemisphere economic readjustments that would stem from the application of further self-sufficiency policies in Continental Europe. The preservation of the British Isles is therefore important in order to minimize the readjustment for the raw-material-producing and raw-material-exporting areas of the Western Hemisphere. That one market absorbs from 30 to 90 per cent of many raw-material export surpluses of our hemisphere. Its preservation, having great military benefits as well as great economic benefits for the hemisphere's export surplus industries, is now a foremost objective of the nations of the Western Hemisphere.

CANADA AND HEMISPHERIC SOLIDARITY

By FRANK SCOTT
Professor of Civil Law, McGill University
Montreal, Canada

CANADA AND HEMISPHERIC
SOLIDARITY

AMONG the American nations Canada ranks first in area, second in economic development, and fifth in population. With the military establishment she has built since the war started, she is unquestionably the second most powerful state in the Western Hemisphere. Yet she is not a member of the Pan-American Union and she does not attend the conferences of American states. What are the reasons for this policy of isolation? Is there likely to be any change under the impact of the present war? And how does her refusal to accept full responsibility within the Pan-American system affect the movement for hemispheric solidarity? These are the topics I wish to consider in this paper.

At the outset let me remind you of certain facts which help to explain Canada's unusual position. She has a population of only twelve million in a territory of 3.7 million square miles. Fully 90 per cent of this population lives within two hundred miles, and 50 per cent within one hundred miles, of the United States border. The demographic shape of Canada is thus a long, thin strip lying east and west across the continent. This strip is divided into four well-defined sections: by the northern end of the Appalachians, by the junction of the Great Lakes and by the Laurentian Shield, and, finally, by the Rocky Mountains. The central provinces, Quebec and Ontario, though both sharing similar economic interests, are divided by race and religion, Ontario being the main center of the Protestant and British influence in Canada and Quebec of the Catholic and French. Of the total Canadian population, approximately 50 per cent is of British origin, 30 per cent of French, and 20 per cent of other racial stock, mostly European. Only 1 per cent are aboriginal Indians and Eskimo. About 60 per cent of the people are Protestant, the rest Roman Catholic. These divisions within Canada make political change slow and make the maintenance of national unity a major concern in the choice of national policy.

Canada, unlike all the other American nations, has achieved her national status by slow and gradual stages instead of by sudden revolution. There is still in existence a political connection with Europe in this part of the hemisphere which has ceased elsewhere. This explains certain traditional attitudes among Canadians toward questions of foreign policy. Political freedom in external affairs has been too recently acquired to have resulted in many changes in the former relationships. It was only after the first World War, and principally as a result of the Imperial Conference report of 1926 and the Statute of Westminster of 1931, that Canada's autonomous national status was acknowledged by international and constitutional law. Indeed, not until this war had actually started, and until Canadian neutrality during the first week had been recognized by President Roosevelt and by the separate Canadian declaration of war on September 10, 1939, can it be said that the final independent right to war and peace was attributed to Canada. But the evolution is now complete, even though Canadians have not troubled to remove certain vestiges of colonialism such as the retention of the appeal to the Imperial Privy Council and the use of the Imperial Parliament as the legal instrument for amending the British North America Act of 1867, Canada's written constitution. What this means, in brief, is that the relation between Canada and Great Britain is now that of two equal and independent countries joined by a personal union under a common crown. If George VI comes to Canada, he is the head of the Canadian state, but if his British government were to come to Canada it would not become the government of Canada. Only Canadian ministers are competent to advise the head of the Canadian state how he is to act with respect to Canada.

The Canadian constitution is a democratic one. It is an ingenious blending of British ideas of parliamentary and cabinet government with American notions of federation and judicial review. The monarchic element in the law of the constitution makes for a more authoritarian and less popular brand of democracy than exists in the United States, but Canadians feel they have achieved a proper compromise between the demand for freedom and the need for order. While some difficulties have arisen with regard to the relations between the central and the provincial governments, these are not so serious as to endanger the constitutional fabric. Canada may fairly claim to have applied democratic principles with considerable success to a scattered and varied population living in a large country.

Canada has already entered the class of the world's great trading powers. In 1937 her total world merchandise trade ranked her sixth among the nations, being surpassed only by Great Britain, the United States, Germany, France, and Japan. Since then, with the decline in foreign trade of other countries and the greatly increased production in Canada owing to the war, she has improved her relative position. Canada's trade with the United States alone went over the billion-dollar mark in 1940. United States trade with Canada is about four-fifths as large as her trade with all of Latin America put together.

Looking at this trade position a little more close-

ly, we find that for many years about 80 per cent of
Canada's total trade has been with the United
States and Great Britain. The United States leads
all other countries as Canada's trading partner; in
the fiscal year 1939 she took 41 per cent of Canada's exports and provided 63 per cent of her imports. Great Britain in that year took 35 per cent
of the exports and provided only 18 per cent of the
imports. North America and Europe took 87 per
cent of Canada's total exports, in almost equal proportions. Since the war started Great Britain's
share of Canada's trade has somewhat increased,
due to the movement of war supplies and the decline of other markets. I shall deal in a moment
with Canada's trade with Latin America, which
amounted to less than 3 per cent of her total trade
in 1939.

Canada's large export trade contains a wide variety of products. The bulk of these are staples,
foodstuffs, and raw materials; in this sense Canada
is still a colonial economy. Gold, newsprint, wheat,
nickel, base metals, and lumber are among the
leading exports. Nevertheless, in the fiscal year
1939 no less than sixty-three commodities were exported to a value of one million dollars and over.
A general view of the distribution of Canadian
trade by destination is given in Table 1.

Industrialization has proceeded far in Canada, a
fact which is reflected in the urban character of the

population; in 1931, 53.7 per cent lived in urban as against 46.3 per cent in rural communities. And though Canada is probably the world's largest

TABLE 1*

DISTRIBUTION OF CANADIAN TRADE BY DESTINATION

(In millions of Canadian dollars)

	TOTAL IMPORTS				DOMESTIC EXPORTS†			
	1937	1938	1939	1940	1937	1938	1939	1940
British Empire........	$236	$186	$190	$ 268	$506	$443	$435	$ 690
United Kingdom....	147	119	114	161	402	340	331	533
Other..............	89	67	76	107	104	103	104	157
United States........	491	425	497	744	360	270	336	417
Europe‡	47	40	37	16	67	75	65	30
Far East§...........	12	8	9	13	33	26	34	17
Central and South America‖	21	16	16	32	25	18	21	27
Other..............	2	2	2	8	6	5	4	7
Total..........	$809	$677	$751	$1,081	$997	$837	$895	$1,188

* *Source: Statistical Summary of the Bank of Canada.*

† Exclusive of gold.

‡ Includes Turkey and the U.S.S.R.

§ China, Japan, Korea, Siam, French East Indies, Netherlands East Indies, and the Philippines.

‖ Includes non-British West Indies and Mexico.

debtor, owing, in 1937, 3.9 billions to the United States, 2.7 to Great Britain, and 148 millions to other countries, it was calculated that Canadians themselves owned approximately 62 per cent of the capital invested in the country as against 22 per cent owned by the United States and 15 per cent by Great Britain.

From the point of view of strategy there are two principal weaknesses underlying the economic position of Canada. One is the insufficiency or absence of the supplies of such vital necessities as coal, oil, cotton, rubber, tin, manganese, steel, and iron. These are serious gaps in Canada's natural resources, and her industrial system cannot approach self-sufficiency. The other weakness is, in effect, the counterpart of her prominent position in world trade; it is her great dependence on overseas, principally European, markets. About 30 per cent of her national income is due to foreign trade. In 1939, 56 per cent of her exports went to Europe, Asia, Oceania, and Africa. Since the economy is so geared to exports, dislocation of her international markets has drastic internal effects. In some areas in Canada particular exports, such as wheat, fish, minerals, or lumber, constitute the sole source of income. The danger in this situation is already evident with regard to wheat. The country now faces a store of wheat that may reach one billion bushels by the time this year's crop is harvested. Present plans for a 35 per cent acreage reduction will not materially assist in a solution of this problem, which will require more drastic treatment if new markets or new uses for wheat cannot be found.

Looking at these underlying factors in broad perspective, two of them stand out as being of predominant importance in explaining Canada's foreign policy. One is her very close geographical, economic, and cultural relationship with the United States. The other is her political, economic, and cultural relationship with Great Britain and the British Commonwealth. Canada struggles to find her own soul amid the pull of these two great English-speaking societies. Mr. Mackenzie King, shortly before this war started, after remarking that Canada's foreign policy must aim first at maintaining the unity of Canada as a nation, pointed out that this policy was made up, in the main, of her relations with the United Kingdom and the United States. Let us see now how the war has affected these relations, and let us look first to Canadian–United States relations, where the most striking changes have occurred.

The close links between Canada and the United States, resulting from geographical propinquity, have been indicated in the figures of Canada's external trade. Similarly close interrelations would be found on an examination of the habits and tastes of Canadians in sports, amusements, education, reading material—and love of summer conferences. This is so clear as not to need stressing. What is perhaps more in need of emphasis is the degree of east-west communication and of contact with Great Britain and Europe, made possible by the St. Lawrence River and the Great Lakes. Without this waterways system a separate country called Canada would scarcely have survived. The strategic aid of the St. Lawrence enabled British sea power first to capture, then to hold, key points at Quebec and Montreal. The economic advantages of the St. Lawrence enabled Canadians to build and to extend to the west a separate economy in the north. But the implied assumption underlying this Canadian east-west traffic was the existence of markets in Europe. So long as those were available—and the imperial connections of Canada, both French and British, made them available —the two national economies, United States and Canadian, were able to develop without any large degree of integration.

Close economic ties there were, of course. Not in forty years has the United States taken less than 25 per cent of Canada's exports or supplied less than 50 per cent of her imports; and the 3.9 billions of United States investments in Canada exceed the British investment. Nevertheless, the two countries remained economically separate and competitive. Canadians showed that, provided other trade channels are open and consumers are willing to pay the price, economic arrangements could overcome in large part the so-called "natural" associations implied by geography. These economic arrangements now fortify the political boundary. To take the simplest example: The Canadian prairies are merely the northern part of the central continental plain which is common to both countries, yet the "artificial" boundary across this plain could not be removed now without disastrous effects upon the United States wheat producers, unless elaborate precautions were taken to dispose of Canadian surpluses. The huge Canadian production is now almost as natural as the central plain itself.

When attention is directed to the strategy of North American geography rather than to the present economic structure, certain other considerations arise. A distant country may make a good market in time of peace, but it may make a poor base for defense in time of war. Strategically, Canada is and must be an integral part of North American, and hence of hemispheric, defense. The very fact that the Canadian-American boundary is undefended makes the defense of Canada's coast essential to United States security in order that her flanks may not be turned by an invader. On the other hand, it is not necessary to stress the importance of United States military and naval aid to Canada in the present world. This mutual need has at last found expression in the creation at Ogdensburg in 1940 of the Permanent Joint Board on Defense. This is a permanent advisory committee of representatives from the two governments. It has no parallel in this hemisphere, though staff conversations have occurred between the United States and some of the Latin-American nations. It has no parallel either in Canada's prior political history, for hitherto Canada's only military commitments have been within the British Commonwealth. Though not called an alliance, the Ogdensburg agreement virtually amounts to one. Further evidence of the strategic integration of Canada and the United States is shown in the acquisition of American bases on Newfoundland and Greenland, extending United States naval operations far into the North Atlantic, and in the building by Canada of a series of air bases in northern Alberta to enable United States planes to reach Alaska overland, thus bringing closer together the two detached portions of American territory on the Pacific. To these military arrangements may soon be added the Alaskan Highway. The long arms of Uncle Sam now envelop Canada on both sides in what may be called a pincer movement except that the pressure is exerted outward rather than inward.

Just as strategy compels new political alignments, so it compels new economic policies. Canada has spent most of her energy since 1867 trying to consolidate her east-west economy and exploring new markets overseas. All attempts to increase the north-south flow of trade by reciprocity treaties failed until the new threats to national security began to appear in the 1930's. Canada even joined, as late as 1932, in an effort to make the British Commonwealth a more integrated economic bloc, but it required only a short experience of what Professor Hancock has called "the period of economic self-insufficiency" to make more sensible policies prevail. In 1935 came the first important Canadian-American trade agreement since 1854, and this was extended in 1938 at the time of the new British-American agreement. Shaken by the world depression and facing new military threats, Canadians recognized the need for more continental solidarity.

Today there are two specially compelling reasons for increased co-operation in trade matters between Canada and the United States. The first is the need for economic backing for continental defense; the second is the joint policy of aid to Britain. It is trite to remark that military plans for joint defense are of little value unless the economic requirements of defense are provided for. The modern fighting man is surrounded by machinery; he is as much a product of the factory as of the barracks. Despite this, the Permanent Joint Board on Defense at first had no economists to assist its military experts. It was not established to do anything else than prepare military plans for joint action in case of emergency. These it has finished and need only

keep up to date. On April 18, 1941, Mayor La-
Guardia and Colonel Biggar, joint chairmen of the
defense board, announced that strategic plans for
the defense of the east and west coasts of Canada
and the United States were complete and that, in
the event of action being necessary, "nothing is left
to be done but to put the plan into operation." It
seems, then, that the military men are well ahead
in their work.

But what of the economic side of joint defense?
Here we may note real progress, but only a beginning. Canada, it will be remembered, entered the
war at its outset and began her separate program
of war production. This had necessarily to be a national effort, for American policy and neutrality
laws at the time made joint effort impossible.
After the fall of France, the scale of Canadian production was greatly increased. The existing peace-
time industries were progressively shifted over into
war production, and new plant was constructed.
The aim was to create not simply a supply of those
materials needed by England, filling in the gaps in
her production, but a well-rounded economic base
for a national defense system, capable of taking
care of the military, air, and naval needs of Canada
in all save the heaviest types of equipment and a
few specialized articles such as airplane engines.
Much of this material could have been more cheap-
ly manufactured in the United States, but, apart

from exchange difficulties, the national plan could not presuppose American collaboration.

Then, as American policy began moving more directly toward active aid for Britain, and particularly after the fall of France deprived Canada of certain British military supplies, the co-operation between Washington and Ottawa grew steadily. Canada had no difficulty in obtaining the additional supplies of raw materials and other goods from American producers that she required for her greatly expanded volume of production, though today priorities must be applied to Canadian as well as to American orders. Providing American dollars to pay for imports was the chief problem, necessitating stringent control of Canadian exchange and a rationing of the available funds. All this effort Canada had to finance on her own, for the neutrality laws prevented her raising loans in the United States. The strain on the Canadian economy was very great. In 1940 Canada's adverse balance of trade with her southern neighbor was approximately $300,000,000, and the British exchange controls made most of Canada's credits on her trade with England unavailable for use in payment of American debts. Unless the United States had made some financial concession, the war effort envisaged by Canada would have been slowed down through inability to maintain the full supply of necessary imports.

CANADA AND SOLIDARITY

The United States did make concessions. In April, 1941, Mr. King visited Mr. Roosevelt at Hyde Park, and the result was the "Hyde Park Declaration," which has been aptly described as the economic corollary of Ogdensburg. By this new agreement, the United States undertakes to buy from Canada certain types of war material which Canada can supply in greater quantity than she needs for herself or for Britain, to the extent of some two or three hundred million dollars annually. In addition, Canada will be provided free under the Lease-Lend Act with materials which her factories incorporate into war equipment exported to Britain and which hitherto Canada has paid for in American dollars. The result is that Canada will sell more to the United States and, while not importing any less, will not have to pay for all she does import. The strain on the Canadian dollars is thus greatly eased though not removed.

From the long-run point of view this joint economic planning is of even greater significance. As between the United States and Canada economic defense, like military defense, has at last been recognized as requiring organs of administration. Last May a joint "Material Co-ordinating Committee" was set up to work out the details of the Hyde Park agreement on commodity exchange, and on June 18 of this year it was announced that economic committees had been established to study and report on the more efficient utilization of the combined resources of the two countries, both during the war and in the period of post-war reconstruction. This term of office may be lengthy. Moreover, a profoundly important principle was written into the Hyde Park Declaration that "in mobilizing the resources of this continent each country should provide the other with the defense articles which it is best able to produce, and, above all, produce quickly, and that production programs should be co-ordinated to this end." If carried to its logical conclusion in an age of total war, such a principle will cut large holes in the Canadian-American tariff. Mr. King, explaining the new agreement to the Canadian House of Commons, said: "Beyond its immediate significance the Hyde Park Declaration will have a permanent significance in the relations between Canada and the United States. It involves nothing less than a common plan for the economic defense of the Western Hemisphere." This language suggests that Mr. King is thinking of economic solidarity over the whole hemisphere. It must be taken as expressing more of aspiration than of fact at the present time, however, for the work of the joint committees is just starting and the two separate national defense programs are well underway. Nevertheless, the trend is plainly evident.

Another indication of economic co-operation is

the revival of the St. Lawrence Waterways treaty. An executive agreement between Washington and Ottawa was signed on March 19, 1941, and now awaits congressional approval. There are two advantages aimed at in the development: an increase of electric power needed for war production and, in the longer run, a twenty-seven-foot channel from the Greak Lakes to the sea, enabling ocean-going ships to enter lakes ports and naval vessels to be constructed in shipyards far removed from enemy attack. In anticipation of this latter use of the waterways, the Rush-Bagot agreement of 1817, limiting the size of armed vessels allowed on the Great Lakes, was amended last March so as to permit heavier construction as long as the ships' armaments are dismantled on the way to the sea. This too will consolidate the two economic and military defense programs.

Thus we see that, under the impact of the war and the new threats from abroad, Canadian-American co-operation has flourished as never before. Canada's solidarity with this hemisphere is obviously increasing at its most logical point. What of Canada's relations with the British Commonwealth? On the political side co-operation has become very close in consequence of the common belligerency. The two countries are allies in the prosecution of the war, and this naturally makes for the closest integration of defense policies. The British

Commonwealth Air Training Plan, which will be turning out 25,000–30,000 air and ground men a year by 1942, is an example of what joint policy may produce. Similarly economic defense plans are co-ordinated to a very large degree so as to produce the most effective results. Canada is a vital source of supplies for Britain, both military and other, and is becoming more so as the full Canadian war program reaches its maximum.

Something of the degree of this aid from Canada to Britain can be gauged from these few statistics. In the fiscal year 1941–42 Canadians will be devoting about 45 per cent of their national income to war purposes; in Canadian dollars, some $2,500,-000,000. Translated into equivalent American terms, taking the American national income at 85 billions, this would total 37 billions. Not only are Canadians financing their own war effort; they now are financing Britain's purchases in Canada to the extent this year of nearly $1,000,000,000. Some of this is paid for by a repatriation of Canadian securities held in England, but the greater part accumulates as sterling balances in London. Canada has now enlisted about 430,000 men in all services. An expeditionary force of approximately 80,000 men is overseas, and Canadians have assumed responsibilities for defense in Newfoundland and the West Indies. Direct income and defense taxes now reach down to incomes of $660 a year, and for a single man earning $4,000 a year amount to $955, or 24 per cent. Governmental controls have sprung up on every hand to co-ordinate the economic effort and prevent inflation. What ten years of human need could not do during the great depression to make governments assume responsibility for social change has been swiftly done by war's demands.

While this huge war effort means close co-operation with Britain, it is being planned and conducted in Canada as a national policy and under Canadian control. It is noticeable that the British Commonwealth has not set up any new machinery of centralized control of policy in this war as it did during the last war under the aegis of the Imperial War Cabinet. This means that the Dominions are more in the position of co-operating allied nations than members of a centralized political unit. Canadian forces in England are under separate Canadian command and cannot be used outside England without the prior consent of the Canadian cabinet. It has been shown how Canada's separate declaration of war—like that of South Africa and like Ireland's neutrality—has emphasized the new kind of Commonwealth which has come into existence, resting on voluntary association rather than on legality. And Canada's need for American supplies means that the more aid she gives to Britain the more she is dependent on those supplies, the more she must pay for them, and the more therefore she must collaborate with the United States in order to handle the financial problems to which this situation gives rise. The war thus has made new Canadian-American relations develop more rapidly than new Canadian-British relations. It must be remembered also that Canada is not part of the sterling bloc. Her currency is pegged part way between that of Britain and the United States. This is having another consequence; it forces other parts of the Empire, like Australia, to cut down on imports from Canada in order to conserve their dollar exchange.

Thus Canada has drawn closer to Britain since the war started. She has also been drawn very much closer to the United States. The two processes have been contemporaneous. This is only possible because American policy has become so actively pro-Ally. Canada is part of a close triangular co-operation.

Thus far I have dealt almost exclusively with Canada's relations with Great Britain and the United States, since these, as I have shown, form the predominant concern of Canadians in regard to world affairs. Anyone wishing to understand what Canadians think about hemispheric solidarity must realize that they approach the question in the way that I have approached it—that is, with the factors I have stressed already in their minds. What now of Canada's relations with Latin America? The concept of hemispheric solidarity, the theme of this Institute, embraces all the American nations. How far has Canada moved, if at all, toward a recognition of the value of a larger degree of co-operation than in the past? The Pan-American group of nations is the only large group in the world among whom there still remains a collective organization similar in essential purpose to the League of Nations, of which Canada was a member. The principles of Pan-Americanism are democratic; they admit racial equality, they respect religious beliefs, they promote co-operation between nations, they exclude force, and they maintain respect for treaties. They are the very principles for which Canadians declare they are fighting in this war. Their disappearance in this hemisphere would be a calamity not only for Canada but for the whole British Commonwealth. Looking at it from a rational point of view, one might imagine that Canada would make a special point, as the only part of the Commonwealth eligible for membership in this group, of joining it and endeavoring in every way possible to see that its great ends are achieved.

This has not yet occurred. But the reason why it has not occurred does not lie in Canada's opposition to the aims of Pan-Americanism; it lies rather in the historical reasons that Canada has been closely associated with another group of nations in the British Commonwealth, that she has only recently come to full nationhood, that Latin America has always been more remote to her than has Britain and Continental Europe, that the Canadian economy is the competitor of Latin America in certain respects, and that the new phase of inter-American development is comparatively recent.

Let us examine these reasons more closely. The Commonwealth relationship has hitherto governed all Canadian foreign policy very strictly. Canadians have desired and have achieved a freedom to choose what policy they want toward all other nations, but they have not wished this freedom to be purchased at the expense of Commonwealth co-operation. To many Canadians—of whom I am not one—it has seemed as though Pan-American co-operation for Canada must mean the end of the Commonwealth tie. They do not seem to trust Canada to be a good member of both groups. Yet it seems to me that as long as the ideals of the Commonwealth and of the Pan-American Union remain democratic, there is no reason why Canada cannot co-operate with both, to her and their advantage.

This fear of outside commitments, in my opinion, is a relic of Canadian colonialism and survives only because Canadian nationhood is still young. Until the end of the first World War, it must be remembered, Canada had not accepted full responsibility for the conduct of her own foreign policy. She never departed from the broad lines laid down by British policy. Her entry as a full member into the League of Nations was considered by many a radical step, and yet this was part of an Empire policy in which the major Dominions joined. Moreover it was understood from the beginning that League sanctions would never be used by any part of the Empire against any other part. Hence the special relationship among the British nations never dissolved into the League system. Thus even the League, though it greatly increased Canada's experience in foreign affairs and did a great deal to educate her people into the responsibilities of nationhood, was not really a complete experience for Canadians of separate, extra-Commonwealth behavior. The Ogdensburg agreement is the first occasion on which Canada has entered into a quasi-political relationship of any importance of her own free will and apart from the Commonwealth group. Joining the Pan-American organization would be another such move, involving even greater departure from past policy. In Canada, with its mixed population and its traditional loyalties, such changes come slowly. Recently there has been, however, one great example of a special relationship between one part of the Commonwealth and an outside power, and that was the offer by Great Britain of union with France just before the French collapse in 1940. If the Commonwealth relationship is flexible enough to permit one part to form a "Union Now" with a European nation, it is certainly flexible enough to allow Canada merely to associate herself, without any political union, with her hemispheric neighbors in the pursuit of common objectives.

Some Canadians have feared that membership in the Pan-American organization would impose a policy of neutrality upon Canada, preventing her from intervening in Europe when she might wish to do so. This objection seems more apparent than real. It is true that a policy of nonintervention in the present conflict was decided on at Panama, but Canada would not have been obliged to assent to this declaration and might even have modified it. Membership of the United States in the Union does not seem to be hampering the Washington policy of all aid to Britain. Canada's defense agreement with the United States is much more likely to limit Canada's freedom of external action in the future, for this involves closer collaboration than does membership in the Pan-American Union. Ogdensburg would already seem to make impossible a policy of neutrality for Canada should the United States go to war with Japan.

Latin America has always seemed remote to Canadians. They have thought of themselves as living as much in the Northern as in the Western

Hemisphere. Latin America is more remote than is western Europe. Even more important than distance is the lack of cultural contact and racial connection. Distance nowadays is not a great barrier to trade, particularly for a country like Canada, with harbors on the Atlantic and the Pacific. The cultural isolation is not so easily overcome. Yet the sense of isolation in Canada is breaking down. There are many influences making for a change in the Canadian attitude. The British Commonwealth is fighting against a desperate foe. Its various members must look carefully to their own security as well as to their aid to Britain. Every step that strengthens the parts gives added strength to the whole. If hemispheric solidarity can be a bulwark against the spread of Nazi power, it should command the support of all Canadians, for Canada's aim in this war is to protect the democratic way of life against the schemes of Hitler. Under the pressure of events, in which the military power of the world seems to be consolidating into great continental masses, the British Commonwealth can no longer afford to be a charmed circle of limited membership. It must look outward to a new alignment of powers and abandon any exclusiveness that might prevent its members from associating themselves with needed allies. Its members have a duty to their neighborhood as well as to themselves.

Moreover, the lack of cultural relationship between Canada and Latin America has been somewhat exaggerated. Many common traditions can be found if people have the will to look for them. Canada, like her sister-nations in this hemisphere, was once a colony and is now a nation. She has inherited certain basic Christian concepts about man and society which derive from the European background and which have hitherto provided some cultural uniformity under all the political diversity of our parent-states. Canada is a small power next to the giant United States; this helps her to understand the fear of Yankee imperialism. Canada has also a large Catholic population, and in the French Canadians she has, in a real sense, a Latin-American race. The law of the province of Quebec is the civil law, not the English common law. These are reasons why Canada, if she chose, could probably find more cultural grounds for co-operation with American republics than can the United States. The recent decision of the Canadian Bar Association to join the Inter-American Bar Association and the decision of the Canadian Federation of Mayors and Municipalities to send delegates to the forthcoming meeting of the Inter-American Congress of Municipalities in Chile are indicative of the trend toward a better interchange of views.

Canada's economic ties with Latin America have naturally been small. Britain and the United

States have been the chief factors in the growth of the Canadian international trade, and they take the lion's share of it. No considerable change in this situation is likely while Canada's war effort continues to direct the bulk of her exports to Britain. Moreover, apart from the war, there are difficulties in the way of any large exchange deriving from the competitive character of the Canadian economy with that of the more southern of the American republics. Canada's wheat surplus is a case in point. In so far as Canada exports manufactured articles, they tend to be competitive in Latin America with those from the United States, in whose branch factories they are often manufactured. To overcome these difficulties there must be a more careful planning of the field, greater commercial contacts, and a furtherance of the work of those organizations like the Inter-American Bank and the Inter-American Financial and Economic Advisory Committee, which are designed to promote economic welfare in this hemisphere. It would seem to be plainly in Canada's interest to support all plans of this character, and it is encouraging to see signs that this is being recognized. Canada has promised to send a trade commission to South America this summer, and she has stationed there some of her trade commissioners recently withdrawn from Europe. Moreover, the diplomatic connection between Canada and Latin

America is being at last developed. Brazil and the Argentine have appointed their ministers to Ottawa, and Canadian ministers will be appointed in return. Discussions with Chile, Peru, and Mexico for similar diplomatic exchanges have been going on.[1]

Figures for Canadian trade with Latin America show a considerable increase since 1938, though they have not yet reached the 1929 level. Broken down for the seven Central American republics, the three republics of the Caribbean Sea and Puerto Rico, and for the ten republics of South America, they are as shown in Table 2.

This table shows that the aggregate of Canada's exports to Latin America in 1940 was 50 per cent over 1938. Trade statistics for the first quarter of 1941 show a further increase, though how long this can continue in the face of the growing shortage of shipping is problematical. The principal commodities exported were newsprint, rubber tires, sewing machines, chemicals, farm implements, potatoes, and codfish; principal imports are petroleum, sugar, coffee, hides, maize, flaxseed, wool, and canned meats.

If we think of Canada's total trade with the Western Hemisphere instead of the trade with Latin America only, then we have a different picture. Including, as we must, Canadian–United States trade and Canadian–West Indian trade, we

[1] Since this paper was read, an exchange of ministers with Chile has been arranged.

find that in 1939 Canada received 68.6 per cent of her imports from, and sent 44.9 per cent of her exports to, this hemisphere. Economically, Canada is more tied to this hemisphere than to any other.

TABLE 2*

CANADIAN EXPORTS TO AND IMPORTS FROM LATIN AMERICA
(In thousands of Canadian dollars)

	1929	1932	1938	1940
	EXPORTS			
Central America........	$ 4,248	$ 1,770	$ 3,146	$ 5,728
Caribbean.............	5,670	1,643	1,978	2,836
South America........	33,759	5,992	12,615	18,305
Total...........	$43,677	$ 9,405	$17,739	$26,869
	IMPORTS			
Central America........	$ 1,195	$ 1,099	$ 808	$ 1,021
Caribbean.............	5,445	891	639	5,535
South America........	26,228	9,941	14,706	27,196
Total...........	$32,868	$11,931	$16,153	$33,752

* *Source: Commercial Intelligence Journal,* May 17, 1941.

As a final reason for Canada's aloofness, I have remarked that Pan-Americanism in its new phase is still a recent growth. Not until 1933 did the active, progressive development of inter-American solidarity really begin. The prior achievements were useful, no doubt, but unimpressive. Canadians had three particular external relationships— with the British Commonwealth, with the United States, and with the League of Nations. These seemed quite sufficient, without adding the Pan-American Union. But with the changing balance of power in Europe, with the disappearance of the League of Nations, and with the steady increase of the good-neighbor policy, the growing collective system in the Americas takes on a new attraction.

Let us now bring together these various threads and see if they make an intelligible pattern. What is Canada's contribution to hemispheric solidarity?

First, we may count to Canada's credit the creation of a stable, democratic order over a very large portion of the northern half of the hemisphere. Canada is a country based on religious and racial toleration, conducting all its affairs by the processes of parliamentary government. It adds greatly to the stability of the American group. There is little fear that the penetration of Nazi propaganda will have any influence in drawing Canadians away from their democratic traditions.

Second, Canadians realize the necessity of preparations for the defense of this continent and hemisphere and are actively co-operating with the United States to that end. They do not think there is any time to be lost in this matter, and they feel that active co-operation with Washington will better preserve their national freedom and honor than will a hesitant and suspicious aloofness. For a powerful security system must be built, and even the small nations have a duty to build it. The significance of the Ogdensburg defense agreement lies in Canada's recognition of this obligation. Moreover, the wording of the agreement is wider than a purely bilateral arrangement would suggest; the defense board, it was announced, would "consider in the broad sense the defense of the north half of the Western Hemisphere." This means more than just the coasts of Canada and the United States. It seems to include at least the Canal Zone and envisages the whole hemisphere. Canada's defense contribution must be measured in terms of her capacities, but the agreement fits easily into the concept of hemispheric solidarity.[2]

By this co-operation, Canada contributes a powerful military weight to the defense forces of the hemisphere. As a country organized for war, she ranks as the second most powerful in the Americas after the United States. Together they form a bloc of one hundred and forty-five million peoples living on what is virtually an island. Between them are one hundred and twenty-five years of peace, and

---

[2] It must be noted, however, that Canada's war equipment is still based on English and not American standards and does not easily fit into American defense arrangements. The Canadian rifle, for example, has a different bore from the Garand rifle.

they have shown that joint administrative agencies can work effectively for the solution of common problems. Their peoples have joint responsibilities for the development and preservation of democracy such as have come to no other continental society in the course of history. I think too, that those responsibilities lie not only outward in the field of external relations but also inward for the enlargement of human freedom and human welfare within the borders of this continent. Perhaps our future New Deals will be joint New Deals.

Third, this military strength of Canada is now being used to assist England in preventing a German victory in Europe. No other American nation is thus actively engaged. Some may perhaps see in this belligerency a breach in hemispheric solidarity. It does mark the difference in political association that exists for Canada and emphasizes the European connection that continues to the north. But presumably the aim of hemispheric solidarity is to keep the hemisphere solid. The chances of its remaining united and increasing in solidarity seem on every count immeasurably greater if Britain wins the war than if she is defeated. Viewed thus, Canada's belligerency is a direct contribution to the possibilities of inter-American collaboration.

Fourth, Canada's contacts with Latin America are increasing and are likely still further to increase. I have mentioned the opening of legations, the growth of trade, and the new Canadian interest in Latin America generally. Mr. King, speaking in the Canadian House of Commons on February 24, 1941, had these words to say:

> South America is likely from now on to have a much closer relationship in business affairs and in matters affecting government and the like with the continent of North America than she has ever had in the past. Unquestionably South American problems will become increasingly our problems as the situation in Europe comes to be changed for better or for worse in the course of the years now beginning. . . . .

Inter-American efforts to dispose of surpluses are bound to interest Canada directly. Canadian businessmen are becoming increasingly concerned over the need for new markets. And from the strategic point of view, the fact that the principle of sharing defense bases has been recognized as applicable by the United States to the bases acquired from Britain as well as to Greenland means that a Pan-American policy now extends to two territories— Newfoundland and Greenland—which are adjacent to Canada. The remoteness of Pan-Americanism is fast disappearing for Canadians.

Fifth, Canada perhaps contributes to Latin America a useful experience of a small country closely related to a great power. The British Commonwealth consists of one great world power, Great Britain, and a number of small powers. The Western Hemisphere consists of one great world power, the United States, surrounded by a number of smaller powers. The central problem of both is how to make the association a democratic one instead of an imperialistic one. How can the parts have freedom in a collectivity which must be largely dominated by the great power? Canadians know a great deal about that question. They took the lead in the changing of the old British Empire into the new British Commonwealth. They might be of real assistance in the solution of similar inter-American problems.

Lastly, as regards the general economic position of Canada, it should be clear that she can never be and would not want to be part of a closed economic bloc in this hemisphere, if such were ever to be attempted, unless she were helped through a truly enormous transition period. The east-west Canadian economy, with its complementary transportation system, designed chiefly to supply more industrialized regions of the world with raw materials, foodstuffs, and semiprocessed commodities, will not easily fit into anything less than a world system. It cannot be fitted now into a Commonwealth system. But hemispheric solidarity, as I understand it, does not aim at exclusiveness but at the strength which comes through collaboration in the pursuit of common objectives. This hemisphere can be sufficiently solid and still have wide contacts with the outside world. Indeed, only thus can it be a help to the world. With such a system Canada may be expected to associate herself ever more closely.

What of the future? Professor Trotter, an opponent of Canadian participation in Pan-American organizations, says:

If the war be not lost, Canadian membership in the Pan-American Union will continue to be inappropriate and unlikely. If the war be lost few Canadians believe that there can long survive any Pan-Americanism which would afford more than transient security for democracy anywhere in the Americas or for nationality in Canada.[3]

I would prefer to say that if the war is not lost a strong and good-neighborly Pan-Americanism will be an essential part of the coming world system, to be integrated with any larger order but not disbanded. Canada will have obligations to this neighborhood, political as well as economic, and it will be her duty to assist in developing a sane, democratic regionalism. If the war is lost, then the survival of international co-operation in this hemisphere is more important than ever, and I do not think it should be assumed that the American nations will easily revert to the status of European colonies. The more we unite now, the less this catastrophe is likely to occur. It may be that full hemispheric solidarity is not yet possible of achievement. It may be that democracy, peace, and the "four freedoms" are also impossible of achievement. But, if a policy be good, the uncertainty of its success is no reason for not adopting it, and in the concept of a democratic solidarity we Americans have an ideal that should command our utmost support.

[3] *Inter-American Quarterly*, January, 1940.

CULTURAL RELATIONS AMONG THE AMERICAN COUNTRIES

By DANIEL SAMPER ORTEGA
President, Gimnasio Moderno,
Bogotá, Colombia

CULTURAL RELATIONS AMONG THE AMERICAN COUNTRIES

THE Norman Wait Harris Foundation, dealing with the improvement of friendly relations among the different countries of this mad world, has very kindly invited me to deliver a lecture on "Cultural Relations among the American Countries." I have nothing interesting or new to say on a topic which your learned professors and writers have thoroughly discussed, stimulated by the discovery the North Americans are now making of the other half of this hemisphere. Nevertheless, it might interest you to learn how we Latin Americans regard your activities concerning our own countries.

I do not want to be unkind. My gratitude to this country, where my father's remains are resting, is very deep. During my two years' stay among you I made very dear friends, from California to Texas and from Colorado to the Canadian border. I traveled fifty thousand miles, stopping here and there to study the true America; the one which lies, far removed from business and politics, among the cotton plantations, in the mountains and along the highways, in the forgotten towns. There I learned that you all prefer truth to compliments, for you are really seeking to make up your mind, rightly and honestly, on this matter of co-operation and to be informed about the whole problem.

I offer in advance my apologies in case my rude English or my rude temper should hurt any one of you. I shall beg your kind attention for some minutes with the friendly purpose of helping you gather all possible information, even the worthless and insignificant.

The theme I am supposed to deal with implies not only cultural relations between the Saxon and the Latin Americas, which is the point directly touching you, but also the relations among the Latin-American countries themselves, a topic in which we Latin Americans, as you may easily understand, are far more interested.

Despite the fact that—with the exception of Brazil—we were born of the same mother, that we speak the same language, and that we have been bred with identical culture, it is a more difficult task to hold our ownselves together than to bind us to North America. It happens that if the friendly relations between the Saxon and the Latin Americas are to be safe and lasting, the first thing to do is to unite the Spanish half of the hemisphere and to raise it as a powerful whole before North America.

Strange as it sounds, this union of Latin America is the only way to close the door to a revival of possible imperialism—the old North American imperialism of the days which we all hope are definitely gone. In the road of our friendship there are certain obstacles, the main ones being: first, the different economic standards of our countries, which make you masters of the markets and make us to a certain degree slaves of your millions; second, the danger of a change in your internal policy and, therefore, of a change in your foreign policy; and, third, the different languages we speak, so divorced from yours, not only in the physical sense of sounds and words but also in the very essence of our appreciation of life.

All these facts bring forth this first plain question, which, in a friendly way and very frankly, I place before you: Are you, North Americans, willing to help us Latin Americans unite ourselves simply because you are idealistic people and because you really trust the principles of democracy, or would your interest wane if you should find in this amalgamation no immediate gain for North America?

Even during the worst times of the old North American imperialism, when Central America, the Antilles, and Colombia, defenseless before the Colossus of the North, had to submit to its violence; in the days when Eça de Queiros analyzed the selfish interpretation that the Senate of the United States was giving to the Monroe Doctrine; when Rodó in his *Ariel* scrutinized the American utilitarianism—even then, I say, Latin Americans distinguished between your government, so much mistaken in its tendencies and practices, and your people, who have always been idealistic, just, and generous, and who condemned with us and as strongly as we did the unwise policy of the "big stick."

Fortunately, your government's policy today coincides with the feelings of the American people. The distrust with which we used to regard you is gradually disappearing. It is true that we are still eagerly sought after by the hunters of concessions; but it is also true that American money and American technical skill are being increasingly applied with good results to the development of Latin-American resources. I do not want to lose this opportunity to say how much I admire the Rockefeller Institute, which has invested so many millions in eradicating from Latin America anemia and yellow fever and has also rendered such good service to this better understanding by the granting of valuable fellowships.

That former understanding of your people which we have from long ago will be a strong force of attraction in bringing us together. The first and most important step to be taken, therefore, should be to acquaint the largest possible number of Latin Americans with the largest possible number of *true* Americans. Not all the visitors we received in the past in Latin America from the United States have rightly represented this great, friendly, and hospitable country. Now, however, we must thank President Roosevelt for his efforts in sending us men truly exemplifying the noblesse of the American thought, the courage, and the common sense that distinguish the mass of your people, of that honest, home-loving, plain, and fair people that is the best in the world.

Allow me to say, however, that, despite your good wishes, those "blitz" trips of your representatives to Latin America are still reflecting the defects pointed out to you by Rodó. We are not given time enough to know and appreciate them nor do they have enough time to learn the truth about us. In my opinion it would be much more effective to spend half the money you are spending but to increase tenfold each visitor's stay in our countries. Frankly speaking, we smile whenever you send us an artist, a writer, or an absent-minded professor to conquer us in a day or to learn in a week all about our psychology, our past, our present, and our future. Social manners in Latin America are different from those in North America; therefore, it happens that, just as we are beginning to get acquainted with our visitors' behavior, they have to return to the United States or to move to another country which they are supposed to study in another week. As a result they arrive back home with a load of misty sensations, and we remain, joking about their attitude.

To change the Latin-American mind toward the United States is a very complex task, the main obstacle being to change your own misconception of Latin-American life.

I can better explain what I mean by comparing the German and the American methods of dealing with us. This comparison has been already made by a clever American teacher who resided in Bogotá for almost three years (Mr. Joe Spear) and who has recently returned to the United States, leaving among us the best possible recollections and many real friends.

Some years ago, Germans used to go to Latin America after having learned their Spanish and Portuguese thoroughly. Americans never gave themselves the slightest trouble in learning our languages: English being the American language, the rest of the world was supposed to understand it or to go to . . . . well, you may complete the sentence.

Germans patiently conquered the Latin-American markets by risking their money and by giving long-term credits to anybody. American methods being different within your own country, you decided that everybody, even the Amazonian tribes, should mold themselves according to the rules previously dictated by the big bosses of New York and Chicago to the American retailers, disregarding the conditions of our markets and never taking into consideration political turmoils, lack of communications, floods, and earthquakes.

Germans went to Latin America to marry there, to remain there forever, to invest their profits in developing new industries and to push forward the Latin-American countries in every possible way. Americans went there to make money as soon and as much as possible in order to return to the United States as soon as possible too, with a hundred picturesque snapshots bound to convince their countrymen how wild, dangerous, and uncomfortable our countries were.

Germans, being imperialistic at the bottom of their hearts, were courteous and *simpaticos* to everybody. Most Americans, being plain and democratic people, generous and idealistic, showed themselves rough in their manners, gestures, letters, offers, questions, and answers.

"Slowly we shall go far" seems to have been the German's slogan in dealing with Latin America, as opposed to your famous "time is money." Rush, rush, rush! This was your initial mistake in the past, and this is also your biggest mistake in the present. You forgot Latin America for centuries, and now you want to win our good will and our markets in a day; but you continue to misunderstand us, thinking that we ought to mold ourselves to your mind and methods instead of trying to mold yourselves to our temperament. The campaign to win our friendship is a rushing campaign too. The old slogan "time is money" still continues to handicap your well-intentioned work to attract us. If I were to define the two peoples, I should say that Germans have been to us like apricots, tender outside and very hard inside, while Americans have been like coconuts: with a heart as soft as butter but very hard in their appearance.

Therefore, it is not to be wondered at if there is a small trend of opinion which in some Latin-American countries leans toward Germany and thinks that a German victory will not be a catastrophe to Latin America. The Germany we knew some years ago was a wise, friendly country; her citizens were all excellent citizens, and they contributed to our country's well-being. Meanwhile, most of the Americans we were accustomed to meet were rough, hurried, and uncultured money-makers.

Thus you are facing a difficult dilemma: it is urgent to acquaint your people with the Latin Americans; but, at the same time, it is important not to confirm the idea they have about your being rushing, eager, and tumultuous—an idea which drove a Brazilian politician to say that, should the United States continue sending them so many ambassadors of their good will, Brazil would declare war on the United States!

But please forgive me for deviating from the

main topic. In order to talk about cultural relations, the first thing to do is to make clear what
should be understood by culture. If a country's
culture is the achievements of her thought and the
permanent work of her mind, culture is represented
by sciences, arts, and literature and by the technique employed in furthering them.

If we start from this definition, we must agree
that the United States is leading, culturally speaking: first, because of her thinkers, to whom she
owes her political organization; second, because her
architecture is one of the greatest accomplishments
of this age, and the United States is writing a new
chapter in the history of this art; third, because in
literature she has developed a medium of her own
—the short story—and because in the field of fine
arts she is far beyond us with her theater, besides
having brought forth a new art quite her own—the
movies.

Of course, on the other hand, Mexico may proud-
ly present herself before the Americas as an original
creator in painting and music; in the latter branch
she is being accompanied by Brazil, which in turn
may teach all of us the technique of the geographical sciences. Other countries, Colombia, for instance, have developed political organizations of
their own, in some points surpassing even that of
the United States, and have created a foreign policy of justice and friendship which influenced your

own nation. Now, then, the question is: How could we profit by your experience and how could you profit by ours?

The most valuable thing you have is your democratic system—the best one in the world, whatever its faults might still be. Meanwhile, the other American countries, excepting Colombia and one or two others, are still halfway or just starting on the road to democracy. Do you think that we might improve them only by giving them good advice? Not at all, because the secret of Latin America's deficiencies lies in her lack of money to educate her masses as you have educated yours. The lack of education prevents us from making the money we so badly need to take care of all our needs. Thus we must arrive at the conclusion that the first practical way of helping the Latin-American nations to organize themselves as true democracies is to help them educate their people.

The investments to be made in this field will not render dividends so rapidly as those made on railroads and oil concessions; yet, they are remunerative, for looking to the future it is clear that the higher the culture and standard of living of our masses, the wider the markets of the American industries.

Coming now to the art of the motion pictures, a creation of your country, as it has been said above, I want to tell you that when the visit of Mr. Douglas Fairbanks, Jr., to Latin America was announced, the newspapers commented upon it by writing that if Mr. Fairbanks' visit was to be a splendid way of conquering the females, it would have been another great idea to have sent us also some of the prettiest girls in Hollywood to conquer the forgotten husbands. At the bottom of this joke there is a great truth: in common-sense language it means that the Latin Americans are waiting to measure the North American's artistic capacity before they will offer their friendship; or, putting it in different words, it means that you should make every possible effort to extirpate a wrong idea long ago rooted there, namely, that you have not yet accomplished your aim of creating in the American masses a true artistic understanding. The Latin Americans continue believing that you are still too much worried about making money to produce good art.

To remove this mistaken idea it would be worth while to present in Latin America the splendid contemporary American theater which, in my opinion, is as good as, if not better than, the best French theater. Unfortunately, it is not possible to present your theater through the excellent actors you have. It must be done through Spanish-speaking actors and through Spanish translations. Nothing pictures the intimacies of life like good theater. The French theater conquered the world, culturally speaking.

Your architecture and your movies are already

reaching the remotest corners of the earth. Unfortunately your short story, like all other written expression of thought, cannot reach us but through books, despite the fine work in this direction that the *Selecciones* from the *Reader's Digest* are now doing in that particular field.

The better circulation of books is one of the greatest problems in the way of our mutual understanding. There are three main fences: first, the various languages spoken in the New World—English, Spanish, Portuguese, and French; second, the high price of the North American books, the ugly appearance of the Latin-American ones, and our lack of a good and organized system of distribution; and, third, the difficulty in our countries of getting money from other American countries with whom we do not have commercial relations. For the time being the American dollar is an international currency. But the dollar being at the same time the medium which enables the governments to square the balance of trade, expenditures which are not imperative—and books are not considered so—are subject to the economic policy of the governments.

Now you have the best industrial implements for book printing, but your labor, though skilled, is expensive and raises the cost too much We have unskilled but very cheap labor; but we have no machinery or technique, nor do we manufacture paper. Why then do we not pull together, each one of us contributing the best he has? American publishing companies could establish branches in the Latin-American countries, the American industry thus selling machinery, paper, and ink and furnishing technical advice, while the countries where labor is not so expensive could help to reduce the cost of the books we all need, getting, in addition, the monetary help rendered by the salaries invested within their own borders. Of course, it would be an essential requisite to eliminate entirely in the whole New World every kind of taxes and barricades to books. If our aim is really to know each other, this point should be the first agreed upon at the next Pan-American conference.

Let us imagine that we have achieved this ideal of printing books with cheap Latin-American labor and the finest American machines and technique. There would be still a second goal: to facilitate their circulation.

Whenever a Latin American wants to buy a book printed in a neighboring country, he has to spend as much effort as if he were building a house. First, he has to discover the book (usually through the American-edited *Handbook of Latin-American Studies*); then he must find out whom to address; third, he has to induce a bank to sell him a minute draft—say, one dollar; then he has to go through all the red tape to obtain an import license from the gold-controller officers; following that, he must risk his work and money when sending it to a bookseller, who very often forgets to mail the book, although he never forgets to keep the money. Once the book arrives, if and when it has safely crossed the turbulent seven seas of not very nicely organized mail services, our man has to start again the red tape and to pay customs, stamp taxes, and municipal fees. Therefore, a book sold in Buenos Aires for fifty American cents will cost a Venezuelan fivefold this amount, plus insurance (without which the book will turn into smoke), plus his time, and plus his liver irritation. If the scholar—who naturally is not a wealthy man (otherwise he would not be a scholar)—chooses to get the book through his own town bookshop, the bookseller, cunning enough and knowing all I have explained, will charge him a commission slightly lower than the cost resulting by the straight purchase.

Among the services that the Pan-American Union is rendering to the New World's cultural *rapprochement*, few are as valuable as those which we owe to its Bureau of Intellectual Co-operation, running under the wise and dynamic direction of Mrs. Concha Romero James. In almost all the Latin-American countries there are committees for intellectual co-operation, integrated by famous writers and politicians who do not attend a single meeting and do not care about such an abstruse business.

In order to make effective intellectual co-operation and to open wide roads to the circulation of books, would it not be possible to establish a branch of the Bureau of Intellectual Co-operation of the Pan-American Union in each one of the Latin-American capitals? Through those branches, being attended to by paid employees, whose only duties would be to carry out the instructions of the main bureau in Washington, we could easily devise ways to avoid the inconvenience at present confronting us. For instance, those branches would issue I.O.U.'s as special currency for book purchasing, such I.O.U.'s to be squared up periodically. Perhaps at the end of each period the governments would have to settle accounts as they do with the mails, using money for compensation; but meanwhile their countries would have enjoyed foreign books that, without a stratagem device like the one proposed, might never be available. Let us inquire into the American technique for the details which might rule this sort of intellectual clearing-house.

The obstacles arising from our having in this hemisphere four different languages are difficult to overcome. But something can be done by eliminating, for the time being, the study of those foreign languages which are not spoken in our hemisphere, in order to concentrate all our efforts, with reasonable and understandable selfishness, in learning those concerning us.

By facilitating the purchase of books and their

circulation among the different American countries, we shall encourage, I am sure, the learning of
our own languages in preference to those of countries on the other side of the world whose books
will be more expensive and difficult to obtain. Let
us say, by way of illustration, that curiosity about
the wonderful American children's literature will
be a force to induce the Spanish-speaking children
to learn English. I cherish the intention of bringing
to Colombia as many American children's books as
possible, in order to keep them permanently before
the eyes of my little countrymen, not with the idea
of doing business but to incite them to study English and, through the marvelous books you have
printed, to give them a better and happier understanding of life.

There are yet two additional good ways to stimulate the teaching of our own languages in our own
world: by broadcasting and by records. Governments could help immensely if they would force the
broadcasting stations to shorten the oral part of
their programs and, at the same time, to broadcast
invariably and persistently all news, advertise-
ments, and explanations in our four languages.
This may seem of little importance, but remember
that dripping water drills the rock.

As to the records, we must seek the mass production of cheap phonographs and of records whose
aim is to teach English, Spanish, Portuguese, and

French. Both machines and records should have no customs duties or taxes of any kind. They should also be freely transported through the mail. It seems too much; but, once the first avalanche had passed, no one would ever remember the present days, which our children will call barbaric. Future generations would not understand how we could have lived subject to so many taxes upon books and implements of learning.

I said at the beginning that it is necessary to unite the Latin-American countries as a whole to counterbalance North America. Once the present war is over, yours may be the only great democracy remaining in the world. What are you going to do, surrounded by opposite systems of government in the other hemisphere, if your only partners and sympathizers are the weak Latin-American semi-democracies? Regard for your own interests dictates that you strengthen to the limit those democracies. It is preferable to have strong friends—even if their strength closes the door to any possible future commercial expansion—than to have feeble sympathizers, unable to help you in a world where violence will be mankind's daily bread.

But how to strengthen the Latin-American countries? Vice-President Wallace has given us a good idea, which, though it seems utopian, is extraordinarily clever: to stimulate by all means their industrial development. If industry invigorates nations and you need strong friends, Mr. Wallace is right.

Strength alone is not enough, though. It is also necessary to consolidate the Spanish-speaking countries and to wean them away from the European influence. This task has to be wisely studied, as the geographical position, sources of living, and the inhabitants are not quite alike in all of them. Those countries within the Caribbean orbit, which sell their main products to the United States and are somewhat in fear of her, are to be attracted by means entirely different from those to be used when dealing with other countries which, strategically speaking, are not linked to North America and are nearer to Europe commercially and which manifest a slightly defiant attitude toward the United States. You cannot expect these latter countries to discontinue their trade with Europe unless you are willing to purchase their harvests, which is an unwise procedure, or unless you help them to replace the European markets with Latin-American markets, even if it means a commercial sacrifice for you.

From this practical point of view there are two good ways to link together the Latin-American nations: the first one would be to establish what we may call a good continental coastwise navigation service, and for this purpose American capital is needed; but, of course, such investment would not give immediate returns. Just think, that in order to go from Colombia to Brazil the cheapest way is to come to New York, despite the fact that Colombia and Brazil have common boundaries. What kind of trade may be expected between two nations subject to the maritime freightage resulting from such an absurdity? Navigation should be established among the Latin-American countries independently from the navigation that at present is linking each one of them to the United States.

The second way to unite the Latin-American countries and the three Americas is to turn as quickly as possible into reality the wonderful dream of the Pan-American highway. A long step toward that goal has already been taken by the United States with the law recently enacted to help the Central American nations with twenty millions for that purpose. But still something more has to be done, because we shall never reach the end while depending upon the achievements of the poorest countries, which at the same time are the ones having the most difficult topography. To solve the problem, each one of the American countries could, let us say, appropriate an equal percentage of its annual budget to be administered and invested by an international committee in charge of collecting the money and of building the Pan-American highway. Such a device would move part of the burden placed by nature upon mountainous and poor countries onto the shoulders of those having better means and larger population, thus apportioning to all of them the efforts we should demand of them, for the richer a country is, the more easily she can contribute to the common understanding and well-being. This solution will help also to avoid technical mistakes. As things are now, the highway's location is subject to the political personal interest of congressmen in each country. Mr. John Doe and Mr. So-and-So do not care about shortening or making cheaper the highway but about being re-elected if it comes down the main street of the towns and cities furnishing most votes. A committee of nations for this purpose should be another one of the points to be brought up at the next Pan-American conference.

But what—you may ask—have navigation and highways to do with cultural relations? Well, cultural curiosity is the result of commercial relations or in any case of some other interest. You are not interested in Abyssinian culture, are you? Italians were, though, and perhaps the English are now becoming interested too. If you are now interested in Latin-American culture, it is because without understanding it you will never master the Latin-American markets. Let us talk plainly at least once in a lifetime.

I approve of your attitude. I approve of it and wish to help you, not only because you are congenial and nice people but especially because our own interest lies side by side with yours.

In addition to the preceding ideas regarding the strengthening of education in Latin America: book circulation, American theater translated into Spanish and performed by Spanish-speaking actors, a thorough use of radios, records, and phonographs, and the linking of the whole Americas by land and sea, there are others. For instance, there are the conclusions adopted by the meetings of educators, librarians, writers, and artists held in Washington in the fall of 1939. On certain points those conclusions coincide with the ideas I have brought to you today and in most cases are vastly superior to my humble suggestions, although in a few cases they are not so feasible as those I am placing before you. I shall not recall that enormous list of agreements, for you all know about them and fear, perhaps, as I do, that they are already buried under a heavy gravestone of boards, councils, committees, sub-committees, leagues, advisers, controllers, and, in brief, the red tape which, curiously enough, characterizes this country, everywhere known as the most practical one in the world.

Leaving the governments to pursue their noble aims through their embarrassed official channels, there are certain other goals easily achievable through private efforts and co-operation.

Schools may interchange teachers, if the country

where the foreign teacher is to live receives board and room and the country sending him pays traveling expenses and his ordinary salary. As director of the Gimnasio Moderno of Bogotá I am ready to carry on such an interchange. In other words, the Convention for Intellectual Co-operation signed at Buenos Aires in 1936 should be privately applied, in as many cases as possible and by as many schools as possible, regardless of the use the governments chose to make of it.

I have heard about the prospect of establishing a Pan-American university somewhere in Latin America. The idea is excellent, but it is difficult to be carried forward, for each country thinks itself entitled to have the university within its boundaries. Let us establish the Pan-American university, yes; but let us work at the same time for true and effective Pan-Americanism when doing so.

As I said above, every country has something to teach to the others, according to her present development, her climate, her traditions, and her history.

Sometimes I like to dream on the topic: "If I were a millionaire, what could I do to improve in a mighty and everlasting way the inter-American cultural relations?" If I had the money, I would apply my efforts to the Pan-American university I dream about, that is, a university spread all over the Americas, having its different schools in different countries. I should place the school of architecture in California, because California is developing a new Spanish-style architecture that fits perfectly into the tradition, needs, and temperament of the Spanish-speaking countries, which are in the majority. The industrial school I should place in Chicago or in Detroit, the commercial one in New York, the school of painting in Mexico, the school of music in Brazil, that of belles-lettres in Colombia, the mining school in Chile or Bolivia, and those of natural sciences and agriculture in countries enjoying a variety of climates, from tropical valleys to those of the snow-clad mountains.

A university of this type is not very expensive, for it is possible to run each one of its schools within a good school of another university already existing. It is a matter of organization more than of buildings. But through a university thus working, a mighty stream of teachers and students would be created; and, thanks to the coming and going of learned people—not in lightning trips but to stay years—permanent and valuable personal contacts would be made, and friendship and understanding among all our countries would swing forward from the field of addresses, conventions, dinners, and red tape to the field of reality.

Do you not think, ladies and gentlemen, that in the fatherland of Ezra Cornell, Johns Hopkins,

Jonas Gilman Clark, and Leland Stanford, Jr., John Harvard, and Eli Yale, it is quite possible to find the man, or the group of men or even an association of commercial or industrial firms of a whole city, willing to pioneer the new Americas— the Americas of the future, the hemisphere of hope, peace, and decency—and ready to link in a lasting manner their names to the hemisphere and to the history of culture?

I am sure that such a man or such a group of men exists, and it is to them I am addressing myself. It is to them I say: Cultural relations among the American countries are to be stimulated by the governments; but only private people having true courage, earnest temperament, and material resources can perform the greatest role ever offered to men of imagination and resolution.

PAN-AMERICANISM AND THE
WORLD ORDER

By J. Fred Rippy

Professor of American History
University of Chicago

PAN-AMERICANISM AND THE
WORLD ORDER

SOME of the most zealous advocates of inter-American solidarity at present are isolationists. Either they have been isolationists for a long time or else they have become converts because they have lost all hope of permanently eliminating Europe's strife. They desire to reduce those economic, sentimental, and cultural ties with Europe which cause the Americas periodically so much anxiety and suffering. They wish to build in the New World a peaceful and secure refuge from the incurable evils of the Old. They believe that hemisphere solidarity is the first line of defense. Holding this view of the world crisis, they are likely to minimize the obstacles confronting Pan-Americanism and magnify its benefits.

On the other hand, a few of the most ardent advocates of participation in the gigantic conflict now raging are rather indifferent Pan-Americanists. They admit that hemisphere solidarity is important as a second line of defense, but they fear that it will interfere with full assistance to the nations at war with the aggressor powers and tend to keep the Americas out of the world organization which they have in mind after the aggressors have been defeated. Holding this view of the world crisis, they are disposed to magnify the obstacles which confront Pan-Americanism and minimize its benefits.

It is a mistake to assume that the desire to create a united America must necessarily be based upon a fundamental longing to withdraw from the rest of the world. In the past many supporters of inter-American solidarity were isolationists. Among the number may be included Thomas Jefferson, Henry Clay, perhaps James Monroe, and certainly James G. Blaine. But that does not mean that such men would be isolationists if they were living today. Jefferson, at least, was keenly aware of the significance of the balance of power in world politics. And Simon Bolívar, the outstanding champion of American solidarity in the early period, was not an isolationist. Bolívar desired, first of all, to create a Spanish-American confederation under the solid and conservative patronage of England because he believed the people of Spanish America could not make the sudden transition from absolutism to full-fledged democracy. He probably intended later to include the United States and Brazil in his confederation; and he envisaged a world league of nations as the ultimate goal. Woodrow Wilson, in spite of the inconsistencies of his Latin-American policy, could be an ardent Pan-Americanist and at the same time the founder of the League of Nations. Several of Wilson's contemporaries in Latin

America—Baltasar Blum of Uruguay and others—were champions both of inter-American solidarity and of a world organization. A number of statesmen of the present day in the Americas have declared repeatedly that their brand of Pan-Americanism does not embrace the desire permanently to withdraw from the world overseas.

The Latin Americans, in recent years, have been prompt to support world-wide efforts to eliminate the use of force in international politics. They welcomed the invitation to attend the peace conference at The Hague in 1907; and, at one time or another, all of the twenty countries to the south were members of the League of Nations. Canadians have the same broad outlook. One might therefore expect the isolationist spirit in the United States to be modified by closer contacts with our neighbors.

Commercial habits of the Americas make isolation difficult. The nations of the Western Hemisphere always have traded with the rest of the world and must continue to do so or suffer serious consequences. No matter which side wins the war, practically every nation within the Americas will be eager to trade in markets beyond the hemisphere, particularly with Europe. Of this fact the statistics for the year 1937 are eloquent proof (Table 1). Dependence on Europe as an export market might be reduced, but the elimination of that market would cause tragic repercussions.

INTER-AMERICAN SOLIDARITY

To the historical and commercial indications that inter-American solidarity is not likely to result in the withdrawal of the Americas from the rest of the world one may add the further evidence of the fundamental principles upon which the New World

TABLE 1

PERCENTAGE OF AMERICAN EXPORTS SOLD
IN EUROPE, 1937

Caribbean nations:		Southern Latin America:	
Colombia	23	Argentina	74
Costa Rica	49	Bolivia	90
Cuba	17	Brazil	49
Dominican Republic	51	Chile	49
Guatemala	27	Ecuador	47
Haiti	64	Paraguay	46
Honduras	4	Peru	52
Mexico	34	Uruguay	60
Nicaragua	32		
Panama	4	United States	41
El Salvador	27	Canada	47
Venezuela	11	Newfoundland	41

movement is based. Whatever may have been the objectives of its champions in the past, the primary aims of Pan-Americanism today are peace among the American states and joint defense against domination or conquest from the outside. But these are not the sole objectives of hemisphere solidarity. Its advocates also hope that the structure they are building here may serve as an example to nations elsewhere. This American movement cherishes no principles which conflict with those held by world internationalists. Briefly stated, its principles and policies, as defined and generally accepted to date, are these:

1. Every nation of the Americas has the right to exist as an independent state, to live its own life, to develop its own culture.

2. No state has the right to intervene in the affairs of another.

3. Nations should have the honor to keep their pledges; treaties may not be modified except with the consent of all the signatory powers.

4. Except in the clearest case of self-defense, force should not be employed as an instrument of international policy; rights and possessions acquired by conquest or coercion will not be recognized.

5. Aggression against any of the independent states of the Americas will be considered as aggression against them all and will encounter united resistance.

6. Transfer of the remnants of European empires in America from one non-American power to another, especially by forceful means, will not be permitted.

7. The American nations will co-operate in the suppression of alien subversive activities tending to disturb the peace within and among them by efforts to thrust upon Americans alien dogmas and modes of life.

8. The nations of the Americas will collaborate in the solution of their economic, social, and cultural problems.

These principles and policies, defined by the statesmen of the Americas, express, we hope, the common interests and aspirations of the American nations. When representatives from these various nations assemble and begin to converse, the discussion is likely to center on difficulties and grievances. We discover more barriers than highways. But no objection should be raised to that. Problems cannot be solved by ignoring them. We shall return to the barriers again even before this address is finished. But, first, let us observe our mutual ties and our vast interdependence.

It is somewhat unusual for nations to proclaim the ideal of collaboration except in critical periods and for specific purposes. It is generally assumed that nations are normally rivals and competitors and must be rivals and competitors. But if this ideal of steady, constant, and long-term co-operation can be followed, it has unlimited possibilities of mutual helpfulness.

The Latin Americans can assist one another and they can assist the United States. Often it is said that Pan-Americanism runs only between the United States and each of the Latin-American states and not back and forth between the Latin-American countries themselves. This situation ought to be changed and will be changed. New avenues of association are being opened now among the nations of Latin America. In the future they will increase.

In accord with the new policy of collaboration, the United States is giving technical and financial assistance to all of the American nations. It is lending and will continue to lend such aid, it is hoped, not with the view of obtaining the highest returns for itself immediately but with the primary aim of helping to solve the problems of the hemisphere.

The gold buried at Fort Knox, Kentucky—a part of it, perhaps, Montezuma's gold, Atahualpa's gold, and the gold of the Zenus and the Chibchas—can be returned at last to serve Latin America. If the gold comes back, we may send it out again. We shall send it out, not to yield 7 per cent for the creditor and another 7 per cent as the spread for the investment banker, but to yield only a modest return, until, with larger profits and higher living standards for themselves, our neighbors shall be able, finally, to supply their own capital, technicians, and managers and attain a larger measure of economic independence.

In addition to the gold in Kentucky, the United States has also a large accumulation of silver somewhere in New York. These accumulations of precious metals are a sort of embarrassment of riches; but in large measure they result from our policy of trying to assist Latin America. The United States buys approximately a hundred and fifty million dollars' worth of commercial gold and silver from eight different Latin-American nations every year. If citizens of the United States own the Latin-American gold and silver mines, the bulk of the profits may go to our own people. Something, however, must be left in Latin America, since our neighbors seem to approve the purchase of these precious metals. What we desire to emphasize is this: our neighbors are eager for development loans

TABLE 2

The Inter-American Export Market in 1937

Country	Percentage of Total Exports		Country	Percentage of Total Exports	
	To Latin America	To U.S.		To Latin America	To U.S.
Caribbean area:			Southern Latin America:		
Colombia........	*	64			
Costa Rica.......	3	45	Argentina.......	8	13
Cuba............	1	81	Bolivia..........	3	7
Dom. Rep........	1	32	Brazil...........	7	36
Guatemala.......	1	64	Chile...........	4	22
Haiti...........	*	28	Ecuador.........	15	33
Honduras........	2	89	Paraguay........	45	8
Mexico..........	2	56	Peru............	15	22
Nicaragua.......	5	55	Uruguay........	13	14
Panama.........	*	91			
El Salvador......	4	61	All Latin America..	10	31
Venezuela........	1	14			

* Less than one-half of 1 per cent. This and Table 1 have been compiled from data furnished by the U.S. Tariff Commission and the Pan-American Union. Fractions of less than one-half of 1 per cent have been ignored in both tables.

and they have hardly any other source of supply save these reserves in the United States. In this respect our interdependence is great. At this point the four- or five-billion dollar investment we of the United States already have in Latin America may be mentioned cautiously. Our investment ties are strong and are bound to become stronger. They can cause irritation and trouble or they can produce gratification and good will. They ought to be a powerful link in hemisphere solidarity.

The same is true in respect to commercial ties. They are strong; they are growing stronger. They are illustrated in part by Table 2, showing inter-American exports during the year 1937.

It is true that the Latin-American countries as a whole sold more than half of their exports outside of the hemisphere in 1937; but they sold 31 per cent to the United States and more than 10 per cent in other American markets. The hemisphere markets have expanded during the emergency, and they can be expanded permanently.

But let us revert to ideals and interests of a less material kind which the Americas may have in common. Although some of these have not been embodied in formal resolutions and agreements, they may be real and effective bonds of solidarity nonetheless. Most of our ancestors came to America to improve their lot and to build a better civilization than the one they left behind. In general, we believe they succeeded. With the heritage they have left us, we wish to continue the experiment; we share a common faith in the New World of opportunity. Our ancestors fought to secure and maintain our independence; we share a common pride in their struggle. The code of morals which all of us accept, a code founded mainly on Christian precepts, is almost identical; we are not disposed to abandon it for the jungle system of might and ruthlessness. We believe in religious and racial toleration, in respect for human rights and human dignity, and in private property and private enterprise adequately regulated in the interest of the local community, the nation, and the international community. And—whether our governments at the moment, from the standpoint of control and operation, be more democratic or less democratic—we share the common conviction that the purpose of all government is the welfare of the people governed.

These mutual interests, convictions, and aspirations ought to be an adequate foundation for hemisphere solidarity. The quest for others may be continued, provided the quest does not cause too much distraction. We have been reminded often that we have little time to spare. In the present crisis, therefore, it may be wise to make a selection among the common possessions we know we have and concentrate on those which seem most vital. In broadest terms, the thing we seek is security: economic security and security against conquest and domination.

In approaching this supremely important objective, we confront certain barriers within our own hemisphere, but we may surmount them by means of intelligence, patience, and good will. Between us are barriers of language, race, culture, economic selfishness, distrust, and exaggerated nationalism. The world crisis demands and furnishes the occasion for their removal.

The language barrier is not so serious as in many other regions. It can be removed and is being removed. In this respect the Latin Americans are meeting the people of Canada and the United States more than halfway. We should improve our pace.

We cannot change our race easily or quickly. But we do not need to change it. We know that there is no pure race, no innately superior race, and no divinely chosen race. We can accordingly curtail our racial pride.

Our cultures are different. But they are not so divergent as they seem and they are destined to grow more similar because the trend is inevitably toward a fusing and unification of all cultures. The peoples of Latin America, Canada, and the United States cannot be classified by means of any neat line separating materialism, on the one hand, and idealism, on the other. A fuller understanding will reveal more cultural resemblances and fewer contrasts.

We know that the profit motive has interfered with hemispheric solidarity just as the profit motive has retarded national unity. It is not easy to effect a fair or satisfactory distribution of the income of economic enterprise among either individuals or nations. Once we supposed the feat was accomplished through the mysterious interposition of a divinity called laissez faire. Now we suspect the process may require a little planned administration. If so, the planning boards may take into account hemispheric as well as national interests and perhaps serve them both. The majority of us are convinced that a fairer distribution of income and opportunity ought to be made and can be made without resort to violence. We must continue to act upon our convictions.

Those who know the history of Pan-American economic and political relations are not surprised at lingering suspicions among the American nations. These relations have too seldom been characterized by moderation and equity. We must leave our neighbors to confess their sins, and we have so many of our own to confess and lament that we cannot undertake even that task now. But we are justified in pointing out once more that the United States is undergoing a genuine transformation which is revealing itself in our conduct as well as in our pronouncements. It is proper also to emphasize the fact that the transformation was not caused entirely by the present world crisis; the transformation began earlier. The time will soon arrive when we may sit down calmly with our neighbors and examine the past. And we ought to examine it, if we wish to do so at all, with judicious impartiality, weighing motives as well as actions, searching for benefits as well as injuries, and viewing the whole in the broad setting of world politics.

Our conduct toward our neighbors may have been nearly as bad as our neighbors have supposed, although we hope it has been a little better than that. Nevertheless, recent events overseas make it easy to visualize tragedies far worse than any we have ever experienced on this side of the Atlantic. And we are now witnessing here in this hemisphere a phenomenon almost unique in the history of the great powers. We are witnessing the recession of the United States from imperialism.

Our Latin-American neighbors wish to escape from what they describe as a colonial status. They are eager to construct a balanced and diversified economy, adding industry to agriculture, mining, and stock-raising. Which of the great powers is likely to raise least objection to that aspiration? Certainly not that militaristic nation with a rigidly controlled economy which seems to be reaching out for world dominance from an industrialized center in the heart of Europe.

Still not wholly convinced of our transformation, our neighbors are asking for official pledges of self-restraint. They are thereby paying us a high compliment. They know that this is an era when the nations which honor solemn contracts are few. But they still have faith in us; they believe we will not violate the treaties we sign. We have given them a number of pledges already. We ought to grant them as many more as we intend to keep. And, in this connection, our neighbors may remind themselves of still another bulwark against unjust treatment. As long as the press and elections remain free in the United States our neighbors may make an appeal directly or indirectly to the people of this country. The recession from imperialism is a popular movement. This situation illustrates the advantages which may be derived by smaller and weaker states from a democratic system in the larger states.

It is evident that the states of the Americas are strongly nationalistic, those of Latin America along with the rest. The spirit of nationalism is a factor which must be recognized. Even the most ardent internationalists would found their world order on the nation-states, hoping that somehow, by measures short of war, they may obtain the consent of such states to the surrender of their sovereignty in respect to certain vital matters of universal significance. And it must be observed that stalwart nationalism is necessary in this crisis in order to prevent a few conquerors from enslaving the rest of humanity. Our dilemma is this: we must have relentless devotion to national independence if we are to check the advance of the "new order," but the very nationalism we require may prevent the collaboration necessary to defeat the aggressors. We may quarrel among ourselves, we may turn chauvinistic and fight one another, and thus fail to create a united front. By refusing to limit our sovereignty, we may lose it entirely. A divided America may suffer the fate of a divided Europe.

One of our immediate difficulties is lack of full agreement with respect to the magnitude and proximity of the peril we confront and the best means of defense against it. Canada has preferred long-range defense and is already in the combat. The United States has decided upon long-range defense by aiding the nations fighting the aggressors—hoping, no doubt, to stop short of war, but at the same time assuming grave risk of involvement in military conflict. The twenty Latin-American nations are standing more or less aloof. Apparently they feel that the danger is not so grave and so near as we suppose or that the best means of defense is short-range defense on this side of the ocean.

They must be conceded the right to make their own decisions. But we should explain to them fully the motivations of the policy of the United States. Perhaps their governments have already received this explanation. In fact, there are probably no secrets about the subject. Our shift from insulation in 1936 to indirect participation in 1940 was sudden but not instinctive or blind. After considerable discussion, the President, the majority of Congress, and probably the majority of the people of the United States reached the decision that the best way to safeguard the nation and the Western Hemisphere was to uphold Great Britain and China and prevent the destruction of the balance of power in Europe and Asia.

We do not approve of the balance of power as a permanent device in world politics. It is too unstable. For many years, in fact, we considered it very wicked. But we believe the system has been an important factor in the security of the Western Hemisphere. The nations of the Americas owe their independence in part to their own military capacity, in part to the Monroe Doctrine properly interpreted and applied, and in part to British policy backed by British sea power. But they owe their independence also in large measure to Europe's strife and Europe's balance of power. The destruction of that balance, the conquest of the British Isles by a mighty military aggressor, would expose the American nations to the greatest menace they have ever confronted. This is what the United States is trying to prevent.

The policy of the United States will have repercussions in this hemisphere. We shall have the problem of priorities in purchases, in sales, in armaments, in ships, in almost everything. The more we buy from Great Britian and her allies the less we may buy from Latin America. The more money we lend or give to the nations fighting the aggressors the less we may lend to Latin America. Thus our neighbors may suffer hardships, and the development of Latin-American and of hemispheric economic solidarity may be retarded. But the motives will be known and, if they are understood, may be appreciated. As the crisis continues we hope we shall receive Latin America's sympathy and assistance. Our objective is the security of the Americas and freedom to continue our experiment in co-operative peace. We believe the experiment may serve not merely ourselves but other regions and the whole world after this tragic epoch has ended.

INDEX

INDEX

INDEX

INDEX

[PRINTED
IN U·S·A]